~ Titles in the Inquire and Investigate Series ~

FORENSICS
UNCOVER THE SCIENCE AND TECHNOLOGY OF CRIME SCENE INVESTIGATION
INQUIRE AND INVESTIGATE
Carla Mooney
Illustrated by Samuel Carbaugh

MUSIC
INVESTIGATE THE EVOLUTION OF AMERICAN SOUND
INQUIRE AND INVESTIGATE
Donna Latham
Illustrated by Bryan Stone

GENETICS
BREAKING THE CODE OF YOUR DNA
INQUIRE AND INVESTIGATE
Carla Mooney
Illustrated by Samuel Carbaugh

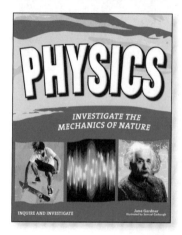

PHYSICS
INVESTIGATE THE MECHANICS OF NATURE
INQUIRE AND INVESTIGATE
Jane Gardner
Illustrated by Samuel Carbaugh

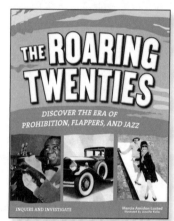

THE ROARING TWENTIES
DISCOVER THE ERA OF PROHIBITION, FLAPPERS, AND JAZZ
INQUIRE AND INVESTIGATE
Marcia Amidon Lusted
Illustrated by Jennifer Keller

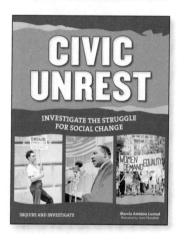

CIVIC UNREST
INVESTIGATE THE STRUGGLE FOR SOCIAL CHANGE
INQUIRE AND INVESTIGATE
Marcia Amidon Lusted
Illustrated by Lena Chandhok

the BRAIN
JOURNEY THROUGH THE UNIVERSE INSIDE YOUR HEAD
INQUIRE AND INVESTIGATE
Carla Mooney
Illustrated by Tom Casteel

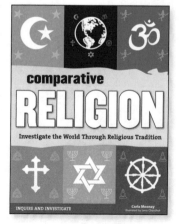

comparative RELIGION
Investigate the World Through Religious Tradition
INQUIRE AND INVESTIGATE
Carla Mooney
Illustrated by Lena Chandhok

Check out more titles at www.nomadpress.net

Interested in primary sources?

PS

Look for this icon

You can use a smartphone or tablet app to scan our QR codes and explore more about the brain! Cover up neighboring QR codes to make sure you're scanning the right one. You can also find a list of URLs on the Resources page.

the
BRAIN

JOURNEY THROUGH THE
UNIVERSE INSIDE YOUR HEAD

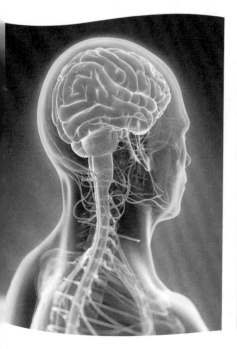
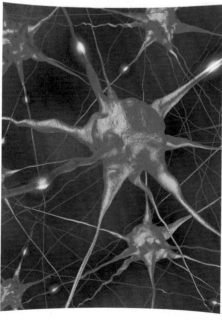
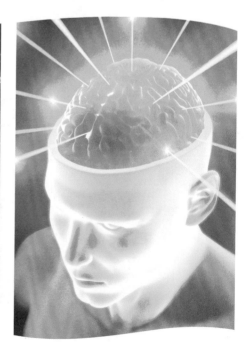

INQUIRE AND INVESTIGATE

Carla Mooney
Illustrated by Tom Casteel

Nomad Press
A division of Nomad Communications
10 9 8 7 6 5 4 3 2 1

This book was manufactured by Marquis Book Printing,
Montmagny Québec, Canada
July 2015, Job #109721
ISBN Softcover: 978-1-61930-278-5
ISBN Hardcover: 978-1-61930-274-7

Illustrations by Tom Casteel
Educational Consultant, Marla Conn

Questions regarding the ordering of this book should be addressed to
Nomad Press
2456 Christian St.
White River Junction, VT 05001
www.nomadpress.net

Printed in Canada.

Contents

TIMELINE

1700 BCE	The ancient Egyptians practice mummification, during which they remove the brain through the nose and discard it, while carefully saving other internal organs.
335 BCE	Greek philosopher Aristotle believes that the brain's purpose is to keep the body from overheating.
1649 CE	French philosopher René Descartes believes that the brain controls some behavior.
1664	Thomas Willis publishes *Cerebri Anatome*, the first book on brain anatomy and function.
1791	Luigi Galvani reveals the electric nature of nervous activity by stimulating the nerves and muscles in frog legs.
1796	Franz Joseph Gall founds the study of phrenology, which links personality traits to bumps on the head.
1848	Phineas Gage is pierced by an iron rod, which passes through his brain and alters his personality.
1861	French physician Paul Broca discovers a language area in the brain, now called Broca's area, which is responsible for speech.
1876	German neurologist Carl Wernicke identifies a second language area, later named after him.
1906	Santiago Ramón y Cajal describes how nerve cells communicate.
	Alois Alzheimer describes the degenerative brain disease that would later be named after him.
1914	Henry Dale identifies acetylcholine, the first neurotransmitter to be discovered.

335 BCE

1861

1924	Hans Berger demonstrates the first electroencephalography.
1934	Portuguese neurologist Egas Moniz carries out the first lobotomy operations.
1936	Walter Freeman performs the first lobotomy in the United States.
1953	Brenda Milner describes patient HM, who experiences memory loss after surgery on the hippocampus.
1969	The Society for Neuroscience is founded.
1970–1980	Brain scanning is developed, giving scientists a new window into the brain.
1981	Roger Wolcott Sperry wins the Nobel Prize for his work on split brains.
1986	Scientists establish the importance of the hippocampus in memory.
1990	President George H.W. Bush declares the 1990s as the "Decade of the Brain."
	Scientists develop functional magnetic resonance imaging (fMRI) to study the brain as it works.
1991	Mirror neurons are discovered by Giacomo Rizzolatti.
1993	Researchers identify the gene responsible for Huntington's disease, a disease that causes a breakdown of nerve cells in the brain.
2013	The United States and European Union begin human brain simulation projects.
	President Barack Obama announces the Brain Research through Advancing Innovative Neurotechnologies (BRAIN) Initiative, with the goal of better understanding the human brain.

1934

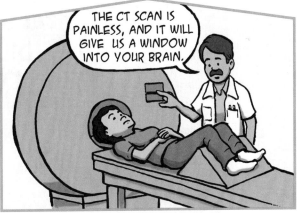

1970–1980

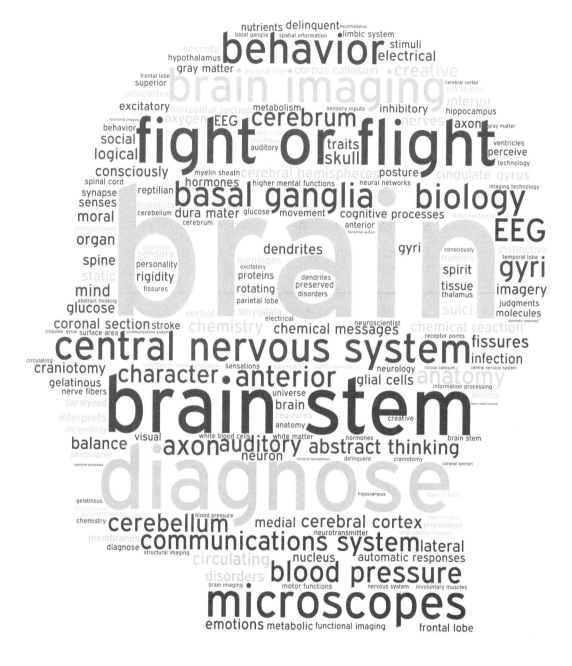

Introduction

Exploring the Mind

WOWZA!

What is the most complex organ in your body?

The brain is the most complex organ in the human body. It might even be more complicated than anything else in the universe!

KEY IDEA

There is a lot of new vocabulary in this book! Turn to the glossary in the back when you come to a word you don't understand. Practice your new vocabulary in the **VOCAB LAB** activities in each chapter.

At first glance, the human brain does not look like anything special. Weighing about three pounds, the brain is a rounded, wrinkled mass. If you could touch it, you'd find that it feels like a mixture of jelly and cold butter. And if you peeked inside a human skull, you wouldn't see the brain doing much of anything.

In fact, you might think that the brain looks very boring. Yet looks can be deceiving. The human brain can do things that no other animal or machine can do.

Without your brain, you would not be alive. Your brain regulates your heartbeat, blood pressure, and breathing. It tells you when to eat, drink, and sleep. Your brain also makes you the person that you are. It guides and directs your actions and behavior. Your brain controls how you feel, perceive, and think about the world around you.

For centuries, people did not realize how important the brain was or why we even have a brain. They believed our thoughts and feelings came from other organs in the body, such as the heart, stomach, or lungs.

For example, ancient Egyptians believed the heart was the body's most important organ and the source of a person's good or evil. When a person died, the ancient Egyptians threw away his or her brain but carefully preserved the heart. In ancient Greece, the philosopher Aristotle believed the brain acted like a radiator to stop the body from overheating.

In 1649, French philosopher René Descartes wrote that he believed the brain controlled some behavior, but that a spirit generated higher mental processes. People still assumed the brain was separate from the mind. Eventually, scientists noticed that people who had experienced head injuries sometimes had behavior and personality changes afterward.

> [Scientists realized the brain and mind were connected.]

In 1796, German physician Franz Joseph Gall concluded that a person's personality and character could be known by feeling the lumps and contours of his or her skull. This belief, called phrenology, links different personality traits with specific areas of the head. Gall said that there were many different personality organs in the human brain, each with its own function and location.

Gall believed that a person's strongest or most dominant traits were also the largest, which made the skull bulge. At the height of phrenology's popularity in the 1800s, some people suggested that politicians should be selected by the shapes of their skulls.

BRAIN TEASER

Since prehistoric times, doctors have drilled holes in the heads of patients to treat a variety of illnesses. Today, a procedure called a craniotomy is used to relieve pressure inside the skull.

BRAIN TEASER

In the 1980s and 1990s, advances in science and technology allowed scientists to study the brain in increasing detail.

Many phrenologists even believed that they could predict future delinquent behavior in children by the lumps on their heads. These ideas have been proven false, but phrenology was important to the development of modern neuroscience.

Because the human eye cannot see many of the brain's parts and processes, studying the brain was very difficult. Through the nineteenth century, scientists could only observe the behavior of people who had experienced brain injuries. To look inside the brain and find the location of brain damage, scientists had to wait until the person died before opening the skull and removing the brain for study.

Today, powerful microscopes help scientists view the brain's detailed anatomy. Electroencephalography (EEG) machines record and measure the brain's electrical activity. Functional brain imaging machines allow scientists to look inside a living person's brain and map its processes as it works.

[With these tools, neuroscientists have been able to create a detailed map of the mysterious human brain.]

Scientists have learned about the brain's anatomy, how it functions, and how it processes information. Technology has shown how the brain sends signals from neuron to neuron and relays information through the body's nerves. We have learned how our five senses turn light and sound input into electrical signals, as well as how different areas of the brain process this information. Scientists have also mapped areas of the brain responsible for memories, judgments, and emotions.

Scientists have made great progress in understanding the brain, but they are only beginning to unlock the brain's mysteries. There is still so much more to learn about the amazing human brain!

The activities in this book introduce you to the basic neuroscience of the human brain. You will look inside the brain to study its anatomy and understand how it functions and processes information. This book will also introduce you to related concepts in anatomy, biology, and chemistry.

You will learn how neuroscientists use knowledge about the brain to diagnose and treat many diseases and disorders. Knowledge about the brain is helping doctors create tools and technology to strengthen and protect our most important organ.

KEY QUESTIONS

- How did scientists study the brain before modern technology? How did this limit their knowledge?
- Why is it important to know how your brain works?
- People were passionate about phrenology when it was popular. Is there anything we are passionate about today that might be proven wrong in the future?

SCIENTIFIC METHOD

The scientific method is the method scientists use to ask questions and find answers. Keep a science journal to record your methods and observations during all the activities in this book. You can use a scientific method worksheet to keep your ideas and observations organized.

Question: What are we trying to find out? What problem are we trying to solve?

Research: What do other people think?

Hypothesis: What do we think the answer will be?

Equipment: What supplies are we using?

Method: What procedure are we following?

Results: What happened and why?

Chapter 1
Brain Structure and Function

What are the four lobes of the brain and what functions do they control?

The brain consists of many different regions, each of which has its own structure and function.

What does a brain look like? How does it work? It turns out that the brain is much more than just a lump of tissue that sits at the top of your spine. The human brain is the center of a complex communications system. It's a communications system that extends throughout your body, all the way to the tips of your toes and fingers.

Our brains receive information from all parts of the body, as well as from the outside world. They process and interpret this information, creating the sights, sounds, emotions, thoughts, and behavior we experience. In addition to all this work, the brain is responsible for keeping the body alive by regulating heart rate, breathing, and other essential functions.

Are you curious about the brain? To develop an understanding of how this amazing organ functions, you'll first have to learn about its structure and how the basic parts of the brain work.

BRAIN ANATOMY

The average human brain weighs about three pounds. Although it may look like a gelatinous mound, the brain consists of many distinct areas, each of which has its own structure and function.

In general, the brain is organized vertically, with higher mental processes taking place in the upper regions and basic life support occurring in the lower regions. All parts of the brain work together, but each part has its own unique characteristics and function.

[
The brain can be divided into three main sections: the cerebrum, cerebellum, and brain stem.
]

The most dominant part of the brain is the cerebrum, a large wrinkled structure that sits at the uppermost part of the brain. It is more than 75 percent of the brain's total volume. Higher mental processing takes place in the cerebrum. The cerebrum also controls your voluntary muscles—the ones that move when you want them to move.

When you plan a vacation, read books, or learn a new language, you are using sections of the cerebrum. Your memory is stored in the cerebrum. Without it, you wouldn't be able to remember what you ate for dinner last night or where you went on vacation three years ago. The cerebrum also aids in reason, helping you decide whether it is better to do your homework now or later.

BRAIN TEASER

The cerebellum is responsible for balance and coordination of movement.

The cerebrum is divided into two halves, the left and right hemispheres. A highway of more than 200 million nerve fibers called the corpus callosum links the hemispheres.

> The two hemispheres communicate by sending messages through the nerves of the corpus callosum.

The hemispheres of the brain are covered with a layer of tissue approximately three millimeters thick. The layer is called the cerebral cortex, which comes from the Latin word for *bark*. Most of the brain's information processing occurs in the cortex. The cortex has a bulging, wrinkled surface. These folds expand its surface area, which increases the amount of information it can process.

The cerebellum is known as "the little brain." It is located at the back of the brain, below the cerebrum. Although it is much smaller than the cerebrum, the cerebellum controls several important functions. It coordinates body movement, balance, and posture. When you hit a baseball or play the guitar, the cerebellum activates.

Without your cerebellum, you would not be able to stand upright, balance, and move around. Have you ever walked on a balance beam? Thank your cerebellum!

Tucked under the cerebrum and in front of the cerebellum, the brain stem connects your brain to the spinal cord. Without your brain stem, you wouldn't be alive. It is responsible for many of your body's most basic functions, such as breathing and circulating your blood.

The brain stem also controls your involuntary muscles, which move without you even thinking about it. Your heart and stomach work with involuntary muscles.

The brain stem tells the heart to beat fast or the stomach to digest food. The brain stem also acts as a relay station for the millions of messages that are sent between the brain and body.

FOUR LOBES

Scientists have divided each hemisphere of the brain's cerebrum into four sections called lobes. The four lobes are the frontal lobe, the temporal lobe, the parietal lobe, and the occipital lobe. Each section specializes in different functions. Because the brain has two hemispheres, it actually has a total of eight lobes.

The frontal lobes sit in the front of the brain, directly behind your forehead. In humans, the frontal lobe is the most developed part of the brain. It receives information from the senses and is involved in high-level functions such as planning, short-term memory, and abstract thinking.

At the rear of each frontal lobe, a motor area controls voluntary movement. On the left frontal lobe, an area called Broca's area works to create language.

BRAIN TEASER

The brain stem controls autonomic processes such as breathing and heart rate. It also conveys information to and from the peripheral nervous system, the nerves, and the ganglia found outside the brain and spinal cord.

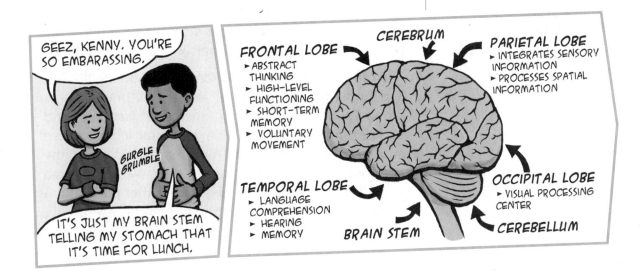

 No two human brains are folded in the same exact way.

Behind the frontal lobes, the parietal lobes are located near the back of the brain. The parietal lobes are involved with the senses. These areas receive information from some of your sense organs to give you details about temperature, taste, touch, and movement. The parietal lobes are also important for processing spatial information such as imagery and rotating objects in the mind. When you imagine how a cylinder would look rotated into a different position during your geometry test, you are using your parietal lobe.

Underneath the parietal lobes lie the occipital lobes. When you look at a picture, your occipital lobes are working. This area processes information received from the eyes and links it to images stored in memory. If the occipital lobe is damaged, a person may become blind.

The temporal lobes rest in front of the occipital lobes and underneath the frontal lobes. This brain area is primarily used in hearing, memory, learning, and understanding language. The temporal lobes receive and process information from the ears. Within the temporal lobe, a specific area called Wernicke's area is used in language comprehension. Other parts of the temporal lobe integrate memories with tastes, sounds, sights, and touch.

LAYERS OF THE BRAIN

Another way to think about the brain's structure is to picture a cake with layers. The brain's top layer is the cortex. Like the frosting of a cake, the cortex covers the entire brain, including the cerebrum and cerebellum. As the most advanced layer of the brain, the cortex enables us to think, store memories, understand language, and speak.

Underneath the cortex is the brain's white matter, or inner brain. The white matter looks white because parts of its brain cells are wrapped in a shiny white myelin sheath. Like a huge satellite network, billions of brain cells in the white matter crisscross and send communications throughout the brain.

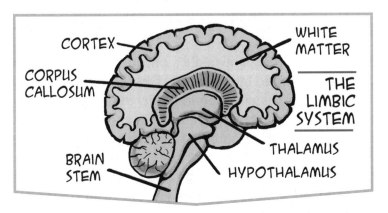

Settled inside the white matter, the brain's limbic system is its center for emotion and feelings. Below the limbic system are the parts of the brain that control growth, hunger, sleeping cycles, and automatic responses.

At the base of the brain, the brain stem attaches the rest of the brain to the body. The brain stem controls many automatic body functions, such as breathing and heart rate. The brain stem is sometimes called the reptilian brain because it is very similar to the brains of lizards and fish and other simple animals.

THE CEREBRAL CORTEX

The cerebral cortex perceives, analyzes, and responds to information from the outside world. It deals with sensory perception and processing as well as higher-level cognitive functions such as perception, memory, and decision-making. The cerebral cortex is made of gray matter and appears as a very light gray color with pinkish and yellowish hues. The nerves in the cortex do not have the myelin insulation that makes the other parts of the brain appear white.

THE LIMBIC SYSTEM

Located underneath the cortex and white matter, the limbic system is a group of brain structures that deals with three important functions: emotions, memories, and arousal. Many of our instinctive behaviors and basic impulses such as sex, anger, pleasure, and fear, which are related to survival, occur in the limbic system. The limbic system links the brain stem, which controls the body's basic life-support systems, and the cerebral cortex, which processes higher thinking.

[
There are several important structures in the limbic system: the amygdala, hippocampus, thalamus, hypothalamus, basal ganglia, and cingulate gyrus.
]

Amygdala: The amygdala produces feelings of happiness, anger, and sadness. One of your strongest emotions, fear, is also generated in the amygdala. The amygdala receives information from your senses, helps the brain recognize potential threats, and prepares the body for fight-or-flight reactions. All of this happens before you even consciously think about it. Do you jump when something startles you? Your amygdala causes that reaction.

Hippocampus: Essential for forming and keeping memories, the hippocampus controls how memories are stored and passes information to long-term memory storage areas. It is also involved in memory recall, which you use when taking a test. If the hippocampus is damaged, a person may not be able to form new memories, even if long-term memories before the injury are unaffected.

A Lot of Wrinkles!

The brain's surface is not smooth. Instead, it is covered with wrinkles called gyri, grooves called sulci, and deeper grooves called fissures. These wrinkles and folds give the brain a much larger surface area of tissue that fits into the small skull. It is similar to crumpling a piece of paper into a ball—you can fit the crumpled paper into a much smaller space than if you left it flat. With a larger surface area, the brain can process more information while still keeping the size of your head manageable.

Thalamus: The thalamus is a relay station for nerve signals coming in from all the senses except smell. This pair of egg-shaped structures sits side by side, sorting the information from the nerve signals and sending it to the appropriate sites in the cerebral cortex.

Hypothalamus: The hypothalamus is only about the size of a pearl. It controls the hormones that enter your bloodstream and make you feel excited, angry, or sad.

Basal Ganglia: These three clusters of neurons at the base of the brain work to initiate and integrate movement. A disease of nerve cells that affects the basal ganglia is connected to Parkinson's disease, a condition that causes body tremors and rigidity.

Cingulate Gyrus: This structure links smells and sights with pleasant memories. It also helps regulate aggressive behavior and is active during emotional reactions to pain.

BRAIN CELLS

Your body is made of cells. Brain cells, however, are unlike any other cells in the body. Brain cells can be classified into two main types—neurons and glial cells.

Neurons are the worker cells in the brain. Everything that happens in your brain is caused by these special nerve cells. Neurons send electrical signals, which cause the sensations, movements, thoughts, memories, and feelings that you have.

[There are about 86 billion neurons in the average human brain.]

Reptiles do not have cingulate gyruses. They tend to be less socially attached to other reptiles and even eat their own offspring.

BRAIN TEASER

In the 2004 movie *50 First Dates*, Drew Barrymore's character suffers from a neurological syndrome that prevents her from making new memories—she relives the same day over and over again, even after falling in love. Can you figure out which part of her brain is damaged?

Some neurotransmitters, called excitatory neurotransmitters, excite neurons and cause them to fire more rapidly. Inhibitory neurotransmitters cause neurons to fire more slowly. The patterns of a neuron's firing creates the different signals that are sent within the brain and to the body.

This fun video gives you a visual idea of how nerve signals can travel quickly.

Although neurons come in many shapes and sizes, most have the same basic structure. The neuron's cell body, or soma, contains its nucleus, which holds and makes the molecules that the neuron needs to live and function. Several dendrites stretch out from the cell like the branches of a tree.

Dendrites receive chemical messages from other neurons. The signals pass from the dendrites through the cell bodies to the axons, which send signals to the next neurons through synapses. A synapse is also called a synaptic gap. Many axons are covered with a fatty myelin sheath, which insulates the axon and helps the neuron's signals travel faster and farther.

At the end of the axon, a small space called a synapse separates the axon from the dendrites of another neuron. Some axons are short and send signals from one neuron in the cortex to another neuron only a tiny distance away. Other axons are very long and carry signals from the brain down the spinal cord.

The brain also has billions of glial cells, which act like the brain's caretakers. They hold neurons in place and protect them. In fact, glial cells create the myelin sheath that protects the axon and ensures its signals are sent correctly. Glial cells also supply neurons with necessary nutrients such as glucose and oxygen. When neurons die, glial cells clean up. They break down the waste and move it out of the brain for disposal.

SENDING SIGNALS

Unlike other cells in the body, neurons don't touch each other. They are separated by spaces called synapses. To communicate, neurons send signals across the synapses by firing a chemical explosion from one neuron to the next.

SO THE GUN'S THE AXON, THE DART'S THE NEUROTRANSMITTER AND YOUR HEAD'S THE NEXT NEURON'S DENDRITES?

YOU GOT IT! NO NEED FOR VISUAL AIDS!

When a signal comes into a neuron from one of its dendrites, a chemical reaction begins in its nucleus, which causes electrical activity. If enough signals are received, a tiny blast called an action potential, or nerve impulse, travels into the neuron's axon and enters the axon terminal.

The axon terminal then releases a chemical called a neurotransmitter into the synapse. The neurotransmitter moves across the space and attaches to receptors on the dendrites of a nearby neuron. The next neuron sends the message from its dendrites down its cell body and the process continues again.

THE NERVOUS SYSTEM

When the brain's neurons send signals, they travel through the nervous system to other parts of the brain and the body. The nervous system is the body's communication network. Electrical signals travel from the sense organs to the brain and back again through its network of neurons.

The nervous system has two main networks. The central nervous system (CNS) includes the brain and the spinal cord. The peripheral nervous system (PNS) is a complex network of nerves that spreads through the body. The CNS and PNS work together to send information throughout the body. If you want to move your arm, your brain sends a message down the spinal cord to the PNS that tells your arm to move.

Messages are sent back to your brain the same way. Sensory input travels from receptor points throughout the body through the PNS to the brain. The brain processes and interprets the information in a fraction of a second, then makes a decision that is sent through the PNS to the muscles, which take the needed action.

LEFT VS. RIGHT BRAIN

Although the two hemispheres look identical, they have different functions. The left hemisphere of the brain specializes in language, verbal memory, and logical thinking. The right hemisphere specializes in sensory inputs, auditory and visual awareness, creative abilities, and spatial awareness.

The brain is wired so that it receives information and sends messages to the opposite sides of the body. The left hemisphere controls the right side of your body, while the right hemisphere controls the left side of your body. If one side of the brain is damaged, the opposite side of the body can be affected.

Watch this fun video and see which side of your brain is dominant.

PROTECTING THE BRAIN

Protecting the brain is an important job. Several layers of bone, fluid, and membranes protect this essential organ from damage. The first line of defense is a hard, bony skull, which is lined with three layers of membranes called the meninges.

The meninges vary in thickness and surround the brain to provide extra layers of protection between the skull and the brain. The outer layer, called the dura mater, keeps the brain attached to the inside of the skull. Underneath is the arachnoid layer, which holds a spider's web of blood vessels that move blood around the brain and then carry the blood back into the body.

The third layer of the meninges, called the pia mater, fits snuggly around the brain like a piece of plastic wrap. Here, blood vessels supply the brain with glucose and oxygen.

Between the meninges and the skull, brain tissue floats in cerebrospinal fluid (CSF). CSF also circulates within the brain. It carries proteins and glucose to nourish brain cells and white blood cells. By cushioning the brain, CSF protects it from being bruised. CSF is produced in the brain's four ventricles, which are spaces in the brain that protect it from extreme pressure.

> Because the skull does not expand, any injury that causes the brain to swell could damage it.

The ventricles allow for small amounts of swelling. Even so, in cases of severe head injury, the CSF may not be able to prevent brain damage.

SCANNING THE BRAIN

Imaging technology allows scientists to study the living brain as it works. This has led to many discoveries about the structure, function, and operation of the brain.

Structural imaging techniques such as computerized tomography scans (CT scans) and magnetic resonance imaging (MRI) take still pictures of the brain to allow scientists to check for changes in brain structure. Functional imaging techniques, such as positron emission tomography (PET scans) and functional MRI (fMRI), show metabolic changes in the brain.

[
These scans allow scientists to observe the blood flow or metabolism in any part of the brain and follow patterns of brain activity.
]

Another type of testing, electroencephalography (EEG), records electrical activity of the brain. Doctors place electrodes on a patient's scalp, which pick up electric signals produced by the brain and send them to instruments that detect the signals and print them onto graph paper.

Doctors can follow the electrical impulses of a patient across the surface of his or her brain and see how changes occur. EEGs can be used to determine how long it takes the brain to process stimuli.

The brain you had as a baby was very different from the brain you have now, and the brain you'll have at age 80 will have changed even more. Brains continue to develop as we grow and age. How they change depends on both our experiences and our genetics.

BRAIN TEASER

Cerebrospinal fluid (CSF) is constantly produced and reabsorbed by the body. Doctors can extract a small amount of CSF to help diagnose certain infections, diseases, or other conditions.

KEY QUESTIONS

- What are the three major parts of the brain? What do they control?

- What are the four lobes and their functions?

- How does the brain communicate with the rest of the body?

- What process does your brain go through when you accidently put your hand on a hot stove?

Ideas for Supplies

- diagram of the brain with sections labeled
- clay or Play-Doh in multiple colors
- tools for modeling
- permanent marker

CREATE A BRAIN MODEL

The brain is a complex organ with a unique, three-dimensional structure. Put your sculpting skills to work to create your own three-dimensional brain model. Using clay, Play-Doh, or another type of moldable material, you can create a whole brain, two separate hemispheres, or sections of the brain.

- **Use the clay to shape different structures and sections of the brain.** How will you use the different colors of clay? How can you make all the sections and structures fit together like a puzzle? Be sure to include the following:

  - cerebrum with its frontal lobes, parietal lobes, occipital lobes, and temporal lobes
  - cerebellum
  - brain stem

- **Add sulci and gyri to the brain's cortex.** What are the best tools to use to create the folds and wrinkles of the brain's surface? Assemble the structures in the proper positions to form a brain.

- **Can you identify the functional areas of the brain on your model?** Include vision, motion, hearing, and memory. What else can you add? Using a permanent marker, label these areas on your model.

> To investigate more, create an inner brain model that includes the limbic system and its important structures, such as the thalamus.

BUILD A NEURON

Your brain is made of billions of neurons that process and transmit information using electrical and chemical signals. A neuron's signal travels through a synapse or special connection with other neurons. Neurons connect to other neurons to form neural networks. Although different neurons process different information, a typical neuron has the same basic parts: cell body, dendrites, axon, myelin sheath, axon terminals. In this activity, you will create your own neuron to help you visualize how it works.

- **Study a picture of a neuron.** Notice where the cell body, dendrites, axon, myelin sheath, and axon terminals are located and how they appear.

- **Experiment with different ways to use pipe cleaners to create a neuron model.** You may want to use a different color for each part of the neuron so that you can easily locate it on the model. Create a cell body and axon. Attach dendrites. Wrap a pipe cleaner along the length of the axon to represent a myelin sheath. Wrap more pipe cleaners on the axon to represent the axon terminals.

> To investigate more, create several neurons and form a neural network. How does a signal flow from neuron to neuron? How can you show this in your model?

Ideas for Supplies ▼

- picture of a neuron from a book or the Internet
- pipe cleaners in multiple colors
- scissors

Ideas for Supplies ▼

- several friends or classmates
- cotton balls

SENDING SIGNALS

Neurons send signals by releasing chemical neurotransmitters across a synapse. This is the space between neurons. The axon terminal releases the neurotransmitter, which moves across the synapse and attaches to receptors on the dendrites of a nearby neuron. This generates an electrical signal that goes to the neuron's cell body. If enough input signals are received, the cell body produces an electrical signal called an action potential, which travels down the axon to its axon terminals. From the axon terminals, neurotransmitters are released to the next neuron.

You can create a model of these signals using a few friends or classmates and some cotton balls.

HOW NEUROTRANSMISSION WORKS

Neurotransmission happens constantly in your body to help you do the things you want to do. Watch this video to see how it works.

- **Arrange your volunteers to represent neurons.** Ask them to stretch out their hands on either side, but leave a gap so that the hands do not touch. Designate one hand as dendrites and the other as axons.

- **Give a cotton ball to each volunteer neuron.** The cotton ball can be held in the hand designated as axons.

- **Simulate a sensory input by tapping the first volunteer.** After receiving the sensory input, the neuron fires its neurotransmitter (cotton ball) from its axon terminal to the next neuron, which receives the signal with its dendrites. How does the signal move from neuron to neuron?

- **What happens when the signal reaches the final volunteer, who represents a muscle?** What should the volunteer do to show that the message was received?

- **Design a neural signal that requires more than one neurotransmitter to fire.** How does it work? What do your volunteers need to do?

> **To investigate more,** incorporate the idea of excitatory and inhibitory neurons. Replace one of the cotton balls with a colored cotton ball or other small item. Tell the volunteers that if they received the colored ball in their dendrite hand, they may not pass it along to the next neuron. Try to send a message. What happens? Why would a neuron want to stop further signaling?

VOCAB LAB

Vocab Lab: Write down what you think each word means: **cerebrum, cerebellum, brain stem, hemisphere, lobes, neuron, axon potential, neurotransmitter, dendrites,** and **meninges**.

Discuss your definitions with friends using real-life examples. Did you all come up with the same definitions? Turn to the text and the glossary if you need help.

SLICING A BRAIN

When scientists study a three-dimensional brain, they can look at it from different perspectives. Each angle allows scientists to view alternate structures and learn new information about the brain.

The coronal section, also called the frontal section, is a vertical slice similar to a slice from a loaf of bread. A horizontal section goes across in the same way we cut a hamburger bun. A mid-sagittal section divides the right and left sides of the brain into equal pieces.

Using a large piece of fruit, you can simulate the different ways scientists slice the brain for study.

CAUTION: Ask an adult for permission to use the knife.

- **Draw eyes, nose, and a mouth on your melon.** This will help you identify the front and back of your brain, as well as the top and bottom of your brain. What are the words scientists use to identify these directional descriptions?

- **Using the knife and cutting board, make section cuts into your melon brain.** Make a number of coronal sections, then make a few horizontal sections. Finally, make a sagittal section.

- **Examine each of your sections.** How does each one reveal different information about the brain?

> To investigate more, try using other kinds of fruit. How are citrus fruits, such as oranges, lemons, and limes, different? What can you see using the slicing techniques on citrus fruits?

Chapter 2

The Developing Brain

How do nature and nurture affect brain development?

Your genes, environment, and experiences influence how your brain develops. Both nature and nurture are important.

Your brain is different from all the other brains in the world. Although all human brains have the same general structure and functions, each develops differently.

What makes your brain unique? Is it the genes you carry inside each cell in your body? Or does your interaction with the world around you affect how your brain develops? Both! The human brain develops from a unique set of genes—that's nature. Your brain is also influenced by your environment—that's nurture.

NATURE—YOUR UNIQUE GENES

Do you have some of the same personality traits or habits as your mother, father, or a sibling? That's because you share some of the same genes.

Inside every cell in your body, a nucleus holds a macromolecule called deoxyribonucleic acid (DNA). It's the DNA that carries your genetic information. Think of DNA as an instruction manual that holds the information you need to grow and function.

Segments of DNA, called genes, control a cell's activities by instructing the cell to make specific proteins. These proteins determine your characteristics and enable you to live and grow.

[
Genes tell the body how, when, and where to make the structures that are necessary for life.
]

Genes are packaged into chromosomes that fit neatly inside the cell's nucleus. Every organism has a specific number of chromosomes in each cell. Humans have 46 chromosomes, matched in 23 pairs, in each cell. You get one complete set from your mom and the other from your dad.

Your genes hold the instructions to make proteins. These proteins play many roles in your body. Genes can turn their activity, called expression, on or off. They can raise or lower their activity. In the brain, gene expression controls the amount and types of neurotransmitters produced by neurons. The neurotransmitters released by neurons affect complex brain functions such as personality, memory, and intelligence.

Some genes may cause the body to make more of certain neurotransmitters and less of others. This can affect a person's brain development. For example, one version of a gene may cause a person's brain to make less of the neurotransmitter serotonin, which affects mood. Having less serotonin might make a person more likely to develop depression. In this way, your genes affect your brain's structure and how it functions, which influences your behavior.

BRAIN AND GENDER

Whether you are a boy or a girl affects how your brain develops and works. Scientists are still studying brain differences in males and females and making new discoveries every year. One thing they've discovered is that parts of the hypothalamus are larger and shaped differently in men. However, there is no clear understanding yet of what this means for behavior.

BRAIN TEASER

Scientists believe that humans have about 20,000 to 25,000 genes. Grapes have more than 30,000.

Brain Map

Scientists are working hard to map the entire human brain. They've started with mice. Brains are so complex that even a very small part of a very small mouse brain gives a huge amount of data for a map. You can see some of the 3-D maps that scientists have made. Why is a 3-D map useful? What can scientists learn from a 3-D map that they may not learn from a flat map?

Your life experiences can leave a long-lasting mark on the genes that affect how your brain functions.

NURTURE–ENVIRONMENTAL INFLUENCES

Think of a bad experience that happened when you were young. Maybe a dog bit you. How did this experience affect the rest of your life? Some people who are bitten by dogs become very afraid of all dogs, even dogs that are small and friendly. This reaction happens because your brain is changed by the world around you.

As the brain develops, it adapts to its environment. Environmental factors can affect how genes express themselves, which in turn influences brain function. Diet, geography, social networks, and stress are some of the environmental influences that can cause chemical tags to attach to a person's DNA. This can alter gene expression, a process called epigenetic alteration.

Scientists have found that mammals that receive nurturing care in early life are better able to handle stress and fear as adults. They believe that the nurturing environment causes epigenetic changes in a gene that codes for a protein that controls the body's stress response. In mammals that did not receive the nurturing care, the levels of this protein were reduced. These animals are less capable of handling stress and fearful situations.

The timing of experience can also be an important factor in brain development. Some experiences are time-dependent. This means that they must occur within a critical period in order to influence brain development. A species of bird called the chaffinch must hear an adult bird song within a certain amount of time after hatching, otherwise it will never learn it.

Other experiences can affect brain development outside of the critical period, although not as much. Children can easily learn a second or third language, often without an accent, but teens and adults have more difficulty mastering another language.

Your genes, environment, and experiences influence how neural circuits are formed and how they function. If a neural circuit is not used, it will not survive or will function abnormally. For example, if you have a vision deficit in one eye that is not corrected in early childhood, the neural circuit that carries information from that eye to the brain will not function correctly and may even shut down.

> [Nature and nurture work hand-in-hand to build your unique brain.]

BRAIN PLASTICITY

At one time, people believed that your brain did not change or grow after birth. They thought that humans were born with a certain number of brain cells and neurons. The only changes that occurred after birth were those caused by injury, brain cell loss, or the natural reduction in brain volume as a person aged.

Today, we know that your brain continues to change throughout your lifetime. Every day, experiences rewire your brain and create new neural circuits, particularly in learning and memory areas. The ability of the brain to change physically is called plasticity, while the formation of new brain cells is called neurogenesis. As you age, the rate of change in the brain slows.

Adults often have a very hard time learning to play a musical instrument.

When you're an infant, your brain is growing and changing at an amazing rate. At birth, a baby has as many neurons as an adult. However, a baby cannot do as many things as an adult because the neural pathways that connect these neurons are not yet fully formed. By age three, there are so many neural connections that they need to be cut back in a process called pruning. Pruning allows the remaining neural connections to work more efficiently.

Some scientists believe that this pruning is why a child's earliest memories fade, a phenomenon called childhood amnesia. They believe that the infant brain does not yet have the sophisticated neural pathways needed to form and retain complex memories.

By age four, the basic structure of the brain is complete. Some parts of the brain have not yet fully developed though and are not yet in use, particularly in areas of the prefrontal cortex.

> At this age, the hippocampus and amygdala have developed enough that memories can be saved.

As parts of the brain mature, different skills and abilities develop. No amount of teaching will enable a child to learn a skill that his or her brain is not mature enough to tackle. Genes control the timetable for learning.

For example, very young children cannot make moral judgments. This is because the prefrontal cortex, the area of the brain that processes these decisions, is

not yet fully working. When the prefrontal cortex is ready to handle these tasks, a child can easily learn the difference between right and wrong.

A window of learning is a period of time when the child's developing brain is ready to develop new skills and functions. If a child receives the right stimuli during this window, they can pick up the skill quickly and easily.

> A child exposed to mathematical stimuli between the ages of about 18 months and five years can pick up math skills more easily than a child who is not exposed to mathematical stimuli until later in life.

THE ADULT BRAIN

The human brain does not fully mature until a person is in their late twenties or early thirties. Around this age, the prefrontal cortex becomes fully developed, which allows a person to be more efficient at processing information and better at controlling emotions and impulsive behavior.

Even when fully mature, the brain does not stop growing. It continues to reform itself, adding new brain cells and changing its connections in response to life experiences. In the adult brain, neurogenesis occurs mainly in the hippocampus, the area that is involved with memory and learning. Neurogenesis in the hippocampus allows you to create and remember new memories.

BRAIN TEASER

In teens, the prefrontal cortex, which inhibits emotion, is still developing. This may be the reason behind the impulsive and rash behavior that this age group is known for.

LEFT VS. RIGHT

About 10 percent of people are left-handed. They use their left hand to write and for tasks that require fine motor control. Studies of the brain have found that people who are right-handed usually have language dominance in the left side of their brains. For left-handed people, about 70 percent have language dominance in the left side of the brain, but 30 percent use both sides of their brains equally for language functions. Some people believe that left-handed people are more likely to be better at visual perception and thinking. Scientists believe that whether a person is right- or left-handed may be determined by genes.

BRAIN JOBS: NEUROLOGIST

Are you fascinated by how the brain and the nervous system work? You might think about becoming a neurologist. Neurologists are medical doctors who diagnose and treat brain and nervous system problems. These include diseases of the brain, spinal cord, nerves, and muscles. Some neurologists research diseases of the nervous system, such as epilepsy or Parkinson's disease, or study topics such as how people perceive emotions.

Myelin acts like insulation on a neuron. It allows the neuron's electrical signals to fire quickly through the axons. If the connections are not maintained, myelin can shrivel, which makes the neuron fire less quickly. Studies have shown that certain foods, such as those rich in antioxidants and omega-3 fatty acids, can help keep myelin healthy.

GROWING OLDER

As people age, their bodies and brains naturally degenerate. Some neurons are lost. Those that remain fire more slowly. This can lead to slower thought processes, memory problems, and problems with balance and movement. Have you ever spent time with an elderly person? How do they move? How do they think?

Research shows that brain volume and size decrease from the age of 20 to age 90 by 5 to 10 percent. In addition, the myelin sheath that insulates neurons decays with age. This causes brain circuits to communicate less efficiently.

To compensate, the older brain may change how it functions. Some studies show that high-functioning older adults use either both brain hemispheres at the same time or a different hemisphere than younger adults or lower-functioning older adults. This adaptation may be the brain's way of keeping thought and memory processes strong even as we age. Regular exercise, enough rest, a healthy diet, and engaging in mental exercises can delay brain decline and age-related problems.

PERSONALITY AND THE BRAIN

Are you shy or extroverted? Are you optimistic or do you expect the worst? Whatever your personality, the answer is found in your brain!

Personality is a group of behavioral characteristics displayed by a person. Scientists believe that many personality traits are linked to specific patterns of activity in the brain. Some of this brain activity is linked to the expression of genes or to genetic mutations.

For example, a person who is an extrovert shows reduced activity in response to stimuli in the neural circuit that keeps the brain aroused. They seek more stimuli from their environment to feel energized. An extrovert may jump on stage to sing in front of the entire auditorium, which gives the extrovert's brain the stimuli he or she needs to feel energized.

Being optimistic is linked to the amygdala and a part of the cortex. When a person imagines positive future events, as compared to negative events, these areas of the brain experience increased activation.

Personality is also affected by environment and how people learn. Personality can be thought of as a person's typical responses to certain situations. These responses can be learned from copying parents, siblings, and other caregivers. They can also be learned from other stimuli, such as television and books.

> If a response is repeated frequently, it becomes coded as a memory and becomes part of the person's personality.

KEY QUESTIONS

- How do genes affect the structure and function of the brain?

- In what ways do environment and experience influence brain development?

- Give an example of your own behavior that is a direct result of an experience you had when you were younger. Why do you have that behavior? What happened inside your brain?

Ideas for Supplies ▼

- a group of volunteers (you can test yourself as well!)
- pen or pencil
- paper
- paper towel cardboard tube
- cup of water
- small, soft ball

BOOP BOOP BOP BOP BOOP

I'M GUESSING HE'S RIGHT HEMISPHERE DOMINANT.

RIGHT VS. LEFT DOMINANCE

The brain is divided into two hemispheres—right and left. Each hemisphere is responsible for specific functions and each controls the opposite side of the body. Your brain's right hemisphere controls the left side of your body and vice versa. For many people, one side of the brain is dominant over the other side. Which side of your brain is dominant?

Try this brain dominance test to find out!

- **Ask each volunteer to perform several tests.** During these tests they have to choose which eye, hand, or foot to use.

- **See which side your volunteers choose to use—right or left—for each test.** Record the results.

- **Here are some ideas to get you started.** But have some fun coming up with ideas of your own as well.

  EYES

  1. Wink with one eye.

  2. Look through an empty tube.

  3. Extend the arms in front of the body. Using pointer fingers and thumbs from both hands, make a triangle shape. Slide the fingers together so the triangle shrinks to the size of a coin. Locate a small object in the room and focus on it through the triangle space, using both eyes. Then close the right eye and focus on the object using just the left eye. Repeat, closing the left eye. When did the view of the object change—when the right or left eye was closed?

HANDS

4. Sign your name.

5. Pick up a cup of water.

6. Throw a ball.

FEET AND LEGS

7. Run forward and then jump on one leg. Which one was chosen?

8. Drop the ball on the ground and kick it. Which leg was used?

• **Review the results from the testing of your volunteer group.** What conclusions can you make about dominance? Were most people consistently dominant for all categories—eye, hand, and foot? Were some people dominant on one side for hand and the other for foot? Were any volunteers ambidextrous— did they use left and right sides equally? Were there any gender differences in the results?

To investigate more, think about whether left- vs. right-brain dominance runs in families. Administer these tests to members of your family and to the families of your volunteers. What results do you find? What conclusions can you make?

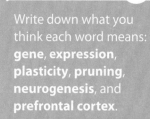

VOCAB LAB 📖

Write down what you think each word means: **gene**, **expression**, **plasticity**, **pruning**, **neurogenesis**, and **prefrontal cortex**.

Discuss your definitions with friends using real-life examples. Did you all come up with the same definitions? Turn to the text and the glossary if you need help.

BRAIN PLASTICITY

Plasticity is the ability of the brain to physically change, forming new neurons and neural circuits, in response to new situations and experiences. In this activity, you will demonstrate how your brain adapts and creates new pathways in response to new visual sensory input.

Ideas for Supplies

- Fresnel lenses or page magnifiers (you can order from Amazon)
- safety goggles or glasses
- scissors
- tape
- piece of paper to use as a target
- measuring tape or yardstick
- masking tape
- 5–10 beanbags
- paper and pencil
- a volunteer

- **When you wear prism goggles, objects appear to be shifted in position.** This occurs because of the way prisms bend light. To prepare the prism goggles, cut two round pieces from the Fresnel page magnifier. Tape these pieces over the lenses of the safety goggles.

- **Place the paper as a target on the floor.** Measure 6 feet away from the paper and mark the floor with masking tape.

* **Have your volunteer stand behind the masking tape line and toss five consecutive beanbags underhand at the target.** The volunteer should do this without wearing the goggles. With each throw, record whether the beanbag lands to the right, to the left, or on the target. Why is it useful in this experiment to toss the beanbag a few times without the goggles?

* **Now repeat the experiment but have your volunteer wear the prism goggles.** Record the results, and whether the beanbag lands to the right, to the left, or on the target. Are there any differences between these throws and the first throws without the goggles?

* **Have the volunteer remove the goggles and again throw five beanbags at the target.** Now what do you observe? Record the results.

* **Switch places and repeat the entire process yourself.** Have the volunteer record your results. Where did most of the beanbags land before wearing goggles? What about with the goggles? What about after you removed the goggles? Why? What does this tell you about your brain's plasticity?

> **To investigate more, increase the number of consecutive throws in each part of this experiment, from five to ten or more. Does this change your results? Why or why not?**

Chapter 3

The Senses and the Brain

How does your brain make sense of the world around you?

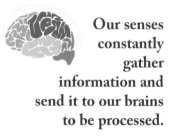 Our senses constantly gather information and send it to our brains to be processed.

If your brain is safely protected inside your skull, how does it get information from the outside world? Your senses! Through sight, hearing, taste, touch, and smell your senses collect information about the world around you. This information is sent to the brain, which uses it to create ideas and reactions. Sensory information is also a powerful influence on your thoughts, emotions, and personality.

SENSING THE WORLD

Sense begins with the sense organs. The eyes, ears, skin, nose, and tongue receive stimuli such as light and sound waves, pressure, or the touch of certain molecules.

Your brain engages with the entire world through your senses. Sensory receptors are special neurons in the sense organs that transform environmental stimuli into electrical signals.

The receptors send the electrical signals to specialized areas of the cerebral cortex. This is where they are processed into sensations such as sound, vision, taste, smell, touch, and pain.

Our senses are constantly gathering information and sending it to the brain. Most sensory signals remain unnoticed or unconscious. Unconscious sensations can still affect our actions and reactions, such as keeping our bodies balanced and upright.

SIGHT AND YOUR BRAIN

From the minute you wake up to the moment you fall asleep, you're watching the world around you. Seeing might seem effortless, but it's actually the result of a long and complicated assembly line that begins with a sense organ—the eye.

Your eyes are actually an extension of your brain. Each eye is made up of about 125 million light-sensitive nerve cells called photoreceptors. When these nerve cells receive stimuli from light waves, they generate electrical signals that are sent to the brain. The signals are processed in the brain and become visual images.

> Light waves enter the eye through a hole in the center of the iris called the pupil. When it is dark outside, the pupil expands to let in more light.

In bright sunlight, the pupil contracts to let in less light. The light waves pass through the eye's lens, which bends the light so that it hits the eye's retina.

The process of sensing the world is a complex interaction between your brain and sense organs.

SENSATION VS. PERCEPTION

Sensation is an awareness of stimuli, such as the knowledge that a smell is coming from the kitchen. Perception occurs when the brain processes that information to interpret what the stimuli means—the smell is coming from a batch of freshly baked chocolate chip cookies. Sensation and perception are both processed in the brain.

Each eye has a blind spot where the optic nerve attaches to it. When both your eyes work together, they can compensate for that spot so you never notice it.

There are about 120 million rods and 6 to 7 million cones in each retina. Rods allow us to perceive shapes and cones are responsible for our ability to perceive color.

The retina is made of layers of light-sensitive rod-shaped photoreceptors and cone-shaped photoreceptors. The light waves are stimuli that trigger the cells of the retina to fire and send electrical signals along their axons. The axons of these cells are bundled together to form the optic nerve.

From each eye, an optic nerve carries electrical signals to the thalamus in the brain. Each nerve carries information from the eye's right and left visual fields. On the way, the two nerves meet at a junction called the optic chiasm, where right and left visual information cross over to the opposite side of the brain.

Fibers carrying information from the right visual field from both eyes combine to form the left optic tract. Fibers carrying information from the left visual field from both eyes form the right optic tract. The thalamus then relays the signals to the primary visual cortex in the back of the brain using a thick bundle of axons known as the optic radiation.

The visual cortex is divided by function into several areas. Each area specializes in a specific part of vision. First, the raw material electrical signal is checked in

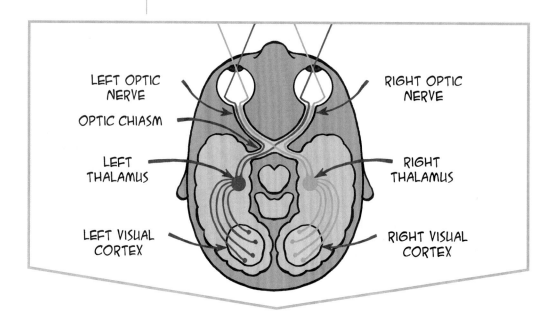

LEFT OPTIC NERVE

OPTIC CHIASM

LEFT THALAMUS

LEFT VISUAL CORTEX

RIGHT OPTIC NERVE

RIGHT THALAMUS

RIGHT VISUAL CORTEX

the primary visual cortex in the occipital lobe of the brain. From there, it is sent to other vision areas that process shape, color, depth, and motion.

[
The brain combines these individual components of sight to form a complete visual image.
]

In order for you to consciously see an object, your brain must also recognize it. To do this, the brain sends visual information from the occipital lobe to the temporal lobe, where it is matched to visual memories and identified, if possible.

Some information travels farther, all the way to the frontal lobes, where meaning and significance are attached to it. For example, when you spot a round spherical object, your temporal lobes identify it as a basketball, while your frontal lobes retrieve your memory of the rules of basketball.

DO YOU HEAR WHAT I HEAR?

Take a walk through town on a Saturday afternoon and you'll hear lots of different sounds—cars honking, people calling, music playing, and dogs barking. How do you make sense of all that sound? Sounds are vibrations of molecules in the air. These vibrations travel through the ear, where they are transformed into electrical signals. The brain then processes and interprets these signals as different sounds.

The process of hearing begins with the ear. When someone speaks, music plays, or a car honks, sound vibrations travel through the air. Your ears pick up these sound waves and funnel them through the outer ear, along the ear canal, to the eardrum, also called the tympanic membrane.

Your temporal lobe identifies what you see. It makes it so you only have to see a chair once to know when a chair is a chair.

CAN YOU HEAR IT?

Why can your dog hear sounds that you cannot hear? The answer lies in the frequency of the sound. A sound's frequency is its number of vibrations per second. Humans can hear and process sounds that fall within a specific range of frequencies, about 64 to 23,000 hertz. Humans are most sensitive to vibrations that fall between 1,000 and 4,000 hertz. Many animals, including dogs, can hear sounds at higher and lower frequencies. The upper range of a dog's hearing is about 45,000 hertz. A whistle that creates sound waves around 40,000 hertz may cause your dog to bark, while you don't hear a thing!

PAIN-FREE LIFE

Some people are born without the ability to feel pain. This genetic condition, called congenital analgesia, occurs because the person does not have pain-sensitive nerve endings in his or her body. Although living a pain-free life might sound good, it can actually be very dangerous. Pain is your body's mechanism to warn you that you are in danger. Without pain warning, a person is more likely to incur severe and even fatal injuries.

These sounds waves cause the eardrum to vibrate. The vibrating eardrum causes several small bones in the ear, called the ossicles, to vibrate as well. One of these bones, the stapes, vibrates against a membrane called the oval window. The oval window passes the vibrations into the fluid-filled chambers of the cochlea. The vibrations travel through the fluid-filled cochlea like ocean waves until they reach the organ of Corti, where hair cells act as auditory receptors and transform the vibrations into electrical signals.

The sound vibrations, now in the form of electrical signals, travel from the ear to the brain via the auditory nerve. Sound information is analyzed in the thalamus. If important, it is passed to the primary auditory cortex.

The auditory cortex sits in the temporal lobe, beneath the temples. Neurons in the auditory cortex determine the frequency, quality, intensity, and meaning of the sound signals, which your brain identifies as sounds.

Louder sounds usually cause auditory neurons to release more neurotransmitters, more frequently. This causes more neurons to activate and the brain to perceive this increased action as greater volume.

CAN YOU FEEL IT?

When you put your hand on your cat or dog's fur and stroke it, what does it feel like? How does it feel to touch a rough piece of sandpaper or a hot stove? How does your brain know the differences between these sensations?

> Skin is the body's largest organ. Your skin has about 20 types of touch receptors that respond to different types of touch sensations.

Touch sensations include light touch, pressure, vibration, temperature, and pain. These receptors are spread unevenly throughout the body. Some receptors register light touch, such as a feathery kiss. Others register pressure sensations, such as when someone squeezes your hand. Still others detect if something is hot or cold.

Touch receptors are linked to a nerve fiber within the body's sensory nerve network. Once a receptor responds to a touch stimulus, it sends information as an electrical impulse via the sensory nerve network to the spinal cord. The information travels up the spinal cord to the brain. Electrical signals travel through the brain stem to the thalamus for more processing. The electrical signal is then relayed to the somatosensory cortex for processing.

The somatosensory cortex curls around the brain like a horseshoe. Data from the left side of the body is processed on the right side of the brain, while data from the right side is processed in the left brain. Each part of the cortex processes data from a different part of the body.

The fingers have the largest proportion of touch receptors in the body.

You don't actually feel the pain from your sprained ankle until your brain has processed these signals as an injury. What seems instantaneous is actually a complicated series of necessary steps.

Sometimes a touch sensation causes you to feel pain. The sensation of pain occurs when specialized, pain-sensing nerve fibers are stimulated. These pain-sensing nerve fibers spread through almost every part of your body.

If you sprain your ankle, the fibers in your ankle send electrical signals to your spinal cord. The signals travel up the cord and cross over to the opposite side of your brain. As the pain signals pass into the brain stem, they trigger automatic body responses.

The thalamus sends the signals to different areas of the cortex for processing. Some areas pinpoint the location of the pain, while other areas plan and execute movement to escape the pain stimulus. Other parts of the cortex work to process the emotional significance of the pain.

OUCH?

Although the brain processes sensory information so that you feel pain in your body, the brain itself does not feel pain because it has no pain receptors. As a result, brain surgeons can operate on the brain while the patient is awake. This is useful to doctors because they can tell if the area of the brain they're working on will affect different functions, such as speech.

WHAT'S THAT SMELL?

Imagine walking into a kitchen where your grandmother is baking a batch of your favorite chocolate chip cookies. Mmmm . . . .

Smell is the most direct sense to the brain. While other senses send their signals to the brain through the brain stem and thalamus, smell signals travel straight into the amygdala and olfactory cortex. Smell signals do not stop at the thalamus first.

> There are about 1,000 types of receptor cells in your nose that allow you to distinguish about 20,000 different smells.

You smell something when the receptors in your nose detect molecules in the air. Each receptor has zones, which respond to several smell molecules. Each smell activates its own specific pattern across the receptor.

When you smell something, scent molecules enter your nose and bind to the receptors. Smell receptors high in the nasal cavity, called olfactory receptors, send electrical impulses to the olfactory bulb in the brain.

The olfactory bulb is located in the brain's limbic system, the brain's primary area for emotions, desires, and instincts. This is why smells are strongly linked to emotion. When you first smell an odor, it becomes linked to the emotions you are feeling at that moment. The next time you smell the odor, it may trigger this link. Every time you smell freshly baked chocolate chip cookies, you might feel the excitement you felt as a child waiting in your grandmother's kitchen.

Information about smells is processed in the brain's olfactory bulb. From there it is sent to areas in the brain's cortex for additional processing. Unlike other sense data, smells are processed on the same side of the brain as the nostril from which the data was received.

TASTE

Your sense of taste often works closely with your sense of smell. Both have helped humans survive. Poisonous substances often taste bad, while nourishing foods taste pleasant. Together, your senses of taste and smell help you decide whether or not to eat something new.

The tongue is the main sense organ for detecting taste. Taste receptors are usually found in groups of about 50, called taste buds. Taste buds on the tongue are most often located in the papillae, which are small protrusions on the tongue.

BRAIN TEASER

Smell is the first sense you use after being born, and we might use it even before birth.

> The average person has about 10,000 taste buds. These receptors on the tongue distinguish between five basic tastes: sweet, sour, bitter, salty, and umami.

Many people who believe they have a taste disorder actually have a smell disorder! These senses are very closely related.

When you eat something, molecules from the food bind to receptors in your mouth, which generate electrical signals. Taste signals travel from your mouth to the thalamus. From the thalamus they are sent to the primary taste areas of the cerebral cortex.

STAYING UPRIGHT

Proprioception, or sensing the body's position and movement in space, is sometimes called the sixth sense. Your muscles, tendons, joints, and ligaments hold your skeleton together. Proprioceptors in the muscles, tendons, joints, and ligaments monitor changes in length, tension, and pressure that are linked to changes in position. Proprioceptors send electrical impulses via the sensory system to the brain for processing.

All of these sensors work together to create an unconscious image of the body's position in space. When the brain processes the signals, it can make a decision to change position or hold still, which is sent back to the muscles as a signal.

Try holding your right arm above your head with your fingers spread apart. Close your eyes. With your left index finger, touch your nose and then reach up to touch your right thumb. Repeat for each of the fingers on your right hand, touching your nose first and then your thumb. Are you successful? Your proprioceptors are helping you accomplish this task!

KEY QUESTIONS

- **How does the brain work with each sensory organ to process information?**
- **How does the brain protect the body using information gathered from sensory organs? Give at least three examples.**
- **If you had to choose which sense to lose, which would you pick? Why? How would that affect your experience of the world?**

TASTE AND SMELL

The chemical senses of taste and smell are closely linked. When one sense is damaged or restricted, the other sense may not work as well.

Investigate how taking away the sense of smell affects how you taste food and your brain's ability to identify certain foods.

Ideas for Supplies ▼

- apple
- potato
- vegetable peeler
- knife
- cutting board

- **Peel the apple and potato.** Cut a small piece of apple, then cut a piece of potato that is an identical size and shape to the apple. Close your eyes and mix up the two pieces so you do not know which one is which.

- **With your eyes closed, hold your nose with one hand.** Eat one of the pieces. Still holding your nose, eat the other piece. Can you tell the difference between the apple and the potato?

- **Repeat the experiment without holding your nose.** How does this affect the way each piece tastes? Does being able to use your sense of smell change how you taste each piece?

To investigate more, repeat the experiment using two drinks. How are your results the same? How are they different? Why?

WHAT'S YOUR PERSPECTIVE? SHEPARD'S TABLES

An optical illusion is an image that is seen in a way that is different from objective reality. What the human eye sees is interpreted by the brain in a way that does not agree with physical measurement of the actual image.

In this activity, you'll investigate optical illusions by looking at a popular optical illusion called Shepard's Tables. It was created by Stanford University cognitive scientist and psychologist Roger N. Shepard.

* **Take a look at the two tables drawn below.** Is one table wider than the other? What do you think?

* **Measure the tabletops with a ruler.** What did you discover? Is one wider than the other? Why do you think you saw it the way you did?

SYNESTHESIA

When the radio plays, you hear sound. But what if you also tasted blueberries? For a person with synesthesia, this phenomenon can be an everyday occurrence. Synesthesia can involve any of the senses. The most common form occurs when a person sees a certain color in response to a certain letter of the alphabet or number. For example, a person might see the word "ball" as red or the number "7" as green. Scientists believe that synesthesia occurs when neurons that send information in one sensory system cross into another sensory system.

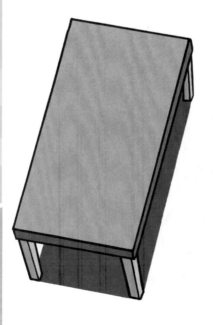

- **What's happening?** As your brain interprets the two images, it is influenced by a lifetime of visual experiences stored in your memory. The German physiologist Adolf Fick demonstrated in 1851 that the human brain is more likely to see a vertical line as longer than a horizontal line of the same length.

Past experiences with perspective cause the brain to see objects as farther away if they are higher on the horizon. In this situation you might even see an object as smaller than similar objects of the same size. You view the vertical table as receding farther into the distance and therefore being longer than the horizontal table. In this way, your brain is tricked by the optical illusion.

> **To investigate more, design your own optical illusion that uses horizontal and vertical lines and perspective cues. Test your illusion on several volunteers. What do they see? How does the illusion work?**

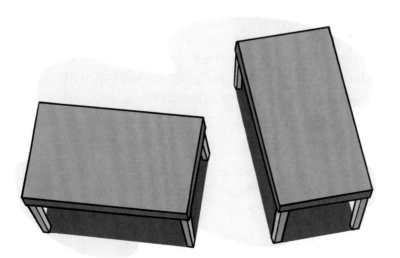

Inquire & Investigate

VOCAB LAB 📖

Write down what you think each word means: **sensory receptors**, **photoreceptors**, **optic nerve**, **ossicles**, **papillae**, and **synesthesia**.

Discuss your definitions with friends using real-life examples. Did you all come up with the same definitions? Turn to the text and the glossary if you need help.

MY GRANDMA WAS A GRATEFUL PHOTORECEPTOR WHEN I GAVE HER MY SCHOOL PICTURE.

Ideas for Supplies ▼

- 2 volunteers
- 2 chairs
- blindfold
- timer

To investigate more, design your own body illusion to trick the brain into perceiving a phantom limb. Test your illusion on several volunteers. How does it work?

BODY ILLUSION: PHANTOM LIMBS

When a person has a limb amputated, he or she sometimes continues to receive sensations and pain from the missing limb. This phenomenon is called phantom limb.

Scientists believe a phantom limb occurs because the somatosensory cortex remaps the way it processes stimuli after limb removal. For example, before an arm amputation, sensory inputs from the arm and hand are connected to specific areas of the sensory cortex. Other body parts are connected to nearby areas of the cortex. After the amputation, the brain no longer receives sensory input from the amputated arm and hand. The pathway to the cortex, however, remains intact. Sensory input from another body part takes it over and sends signals to the cortex. These signals produce sensations in the brain even though the arm is no longer there.

In this activity, try to trick your brain and create the feeling of a phantom limb.

- **Sit on a chair and put on the blindfold.** Have one volunteer sit on a chair in front of you, with his or her back to you.

- **Have the second volunteer take your right hand and place it on the first volunteer's nose.** Gently stroke the volunteer's nose. At the same time, make identical movements on your own nose with your left hand. Continue for 60 seconds.

- **Immediately after you stop, try to touch your own nose with your right hand.** What happens?

- **Repeat the experiment, giving each volunteer a chance to be blindfolded.** How do their experiences compare to yours?

FADING SMELLS

Have you ever noticed that when you are around a smell for a long time, it seems to fade away and you can no longer smell it? Maybe you notice a "doggy" smell when you visit your friend's house, but not your own. Or the smell of dinner cooking in the kitchen seems stronger when you first walk in, but fades as you sit down to eat.

In this activity, you will experiment with olfactory fatigue. Testing different items, you will see how long it takes for the scent to fade away.

- **Put a little bit of each test item into separate plastic containers.** Seal the lids firmly.

- **You need to make sure no smells are present that could affect your results.** Conduct your test in a separate room and ask the volunteers to wait outside the testing room until it's their turn.

- **Have the first volunteer open one container.** The volunteer should hold it approximately 6 to 8 inches from his or her nose. Start the timer when the volunteer begins to gently inhale the scent. Stop the timer when the volunteer says that he or she can no longer detect the scent. Replace the lid on the container and record your results.

- **Wait five minutes.** Have the volunteer drink a few sips of water to clear his or her nose. Then repeat the procedure with a second test item. Continue waiting and repeating for all test items. Time and record the results.

- **When you have finished testing all the volunteers, analyze your data.** What results did you find? How do you explain your findings? Try analyzing your data by gender or age. What conclusions can you make?

Ideas for Supplies ▼

- several small plastic containers with lids
- 4 items to smell, such as peppermint oil, fresh-ground coffee, cinnamon, and tuna fish
- timer
- paper and pencil
- several volunteers

To investigate more, change the scent items you test. Do the different items change your results? What if you mix two items together? Does it affect your results?

Chapter 4

Emotions and Feelings

Why does your heart beat faster and your breathing rate increase when you are scared?

Your emotions help you identify and take care of your survival needs, such as running away when you're scared.

Fear. Joy. Sadness. Anger. You experience many emotions every day. Why do you have emotions? What causes emotions? And what is your brain's role in generating emotions?

Your senses send your brain information about the outside world. Your emotions help you understand what this information means to you. Emotions motivate a person to take care of basic needs for survival. Just as thirst motivates you to find water, emotions motivate you to take care of other survival needs, such as safety and companionship.

Brain scans have shown that positive emotions are generally linked to the brain's left hemisphere, while negative emotions are linked to the right hemisphere.

WHAT ARE EMOTIONS?

In their simplest form, emotions are bodily changes that cause you to act. The emotion of fear causes you to move away from something dangerous, while pleasure drives you toward a reward.

Although it may not seem like it, you are unaware of most of your emotions. But emotions are constantly produced by your brain and body.

There are six main categories of emotion—fear, anger, sadness, joy, surprise, and disgust. These emotions can be recognized worldwide, regardless of country, culture, age, or gender. Looking at a stranger from halfway around the world, you can probably recognize from his body movement and facial expression if he is happy or angry.

Emotions can be shown outwardly through visible changes in the body. Muscle contractions, blood vessel dilations, and facial expressions communicate the emotions you feel without you having to say a word. For example, anger and fear set your heart racing, while happiness makes you smile.

> What happens to your face when you're surprised? When you're disgusted? Can you prevent your facial expression from changing when you imagine smelling something terrible?

Every day, your emotions help you plan and manage your life. Emotions and decision making are closely linked in the brain. Have you ever had a "gut feeling" about something? You were probably unconsciously processing information from the outside world, which was causing an emotional reaction. This emotional reaction tells you what to do.

Scientists have found that when people suffer damage to the front of their brains, they sometimes experience damage to both their emotions and decision-making skills.

EATING THAT SANDWICH MADE ME HAPPY, BUT NOW IT'S GONE AND I'M SAD

VISITING THE BRAIN LAB IS GOING TO PUT ME IN A GOOD MOOD FOR DAYS.

PHINEAS GAGE

In 1848, an American railroad worker named Phineas Gage was injured when an explosion sent a large iron rod through his head. Much of his brain's left frontal lobe was damaged in the accident. Although Gage survived, his behavior changed dramatically. Before the accident, Gage was polite and thoughtful. After the accident, he was rude and reckless. Friends of Gage said that he was no longer the same person.

Doctors believe that the changes in Gage's personality were a result of brain damage. His case was one of the first to demonstrate that brain damage to the frontal lobes can affect social and moral judgment. Decades later, a reconstruction of Gage's injuries showed that the areas of his brain linked to moral sensitivity were damaged in his accident.

No single area of your brain is responsible for processing all emotions. There are several brain areas and neural networks that deal with emotions. Most of the brain's emotional processing is centered in the limbic system. The limbic system is located underneath the cortex and contains several structures that are involved in emotion, including the thalamus, amygdala, and hippocampus.

Neurotransmitters in the brain play a large role in the emotions you feel. At any point, there are dozens of chemical neurotransmitters active in your brain. Some carry messages from neuron to neuron, while others send messages to entire regions of the brain.

[Combinations of neurotransmitters allow your brain to adjust how it responds to stimuli and change your emotions.]

If you see a dangerous snake, your brain releases neurotransmitters that allow you to react fast and move to safety. When the danger passes, your brain releases calming neurotransmitters that slow down the response in the regions that process fear.

FEAR RESPONSE

Have you ever spotted a spider swooshing down from its web on the ceiling and jumped to the other side of the room before even deciding to move? That's an example of your brain watching out for you!

Your brain reacts to scary things before you even know you should be scared. Your amygdala allows you to react almost instantaneously to danger.

> This is because fear triggers immediate changes in the body. Your hair stands on end, your heart beats faster, and your body gets ready to either attack or run.

Your amygdala sends signals to parts of your brain that enable your body to react quickly to the sight or sound of danger. The fast response of the amygdala gives you the seconds you need to survive if the threat turns out to be real.

At the same time, that same information—the sight of the spider—travels more slowly from the thalamus to the cortex, where it is evaluated. This is where other experiences you may have had with spiders, both good and bad, are compared to your current experience. If the threat is not real, the cortex will overrule the amygdala and send signals to lower the body's fight-or-flight response.

Infants are born knowing how to express certain emotions, including sadness and joy—they laugh and cry at birth or soon afterward.

All mammals process basic emotions such as fear and anger. Humans also have social emotions such as shame, guilt, and pride, which are based on being aware of what other people think about them.

ACH!! MONSTER!!

*AMYGDALA: DANGER! SCREAM AND RUN AWAY!

WHEW! IT'S JUST A MOP

YEAH, YOU STILL NEED TO HELP CLEAN UP THE LAB.

*CORTEX: CALM DOWN! THAT'S NOT A MONSTER.

AHHH!!

*AMYGDALA: RUN AWAY!
**CORTEX: CLEANING? THREAT CONFIRMED! KEEP RUNNING!

You show emotion in your facial expressions and in your body movements. Often, you aren't even aware of the changes that occur when a rush of emotion surges through your body.

A rush of adrenaline causes you to tremble when you're scared, which loosens your muscles and organs to prepare for fight or flight. You might blush when angry because adrenaline dilates the blood vessels near the skin, flushing your face and neck. This adrenaline is useful because it gives you an extra surge of energy. Some scientists believe that blushing also makes other people more sympathetic to your cause—if you blush, other people are more likely to take your side.

> Do you cry when you're sad? Your tears remove chemicals such as manganese, which lowers stress in your body.

Humans make unconscious expressions on their faces when they feel certain emotions. Two nerves that originate in the brain stem control the muscles that create facial expressions. The neurons that control these facial muscles receive signals from the cortex and the limbic areas of the brain. The limbic areas and autonomic nervous system send signals that cause fast, involuntary facial movements in response to emotional stimuli, such as your eyes widening in fear or your mouth dropping open in surprise.

The cortex, however, sends signals that control voluntary facial movements. These signals can suppress the involuntary expressions, such as when you quickly shut your mouth to pretend that you were not surprised at all!

3-D MODELS

Many people understand concepts best when they can visualize these concepts. That's why scientists create 3-D models of how communication within the brain works. Do you understand things better if you can see models? Why?

BRAIN TEASER

Most emotions are sudden, intense reactions that last for only a few hours. In some cases, however, emotions can lead to a longer-lasting condition called mood. Your mood is your state of mind or predominant emotion. Moods can last for hours, days, or even months.

PERCEIVING EMOTIONS

We learn to recognize emotions in the people around us at an early age. Babies as young as four months have been found to pick up on the nonverbal cues humans use for communication, such as upturned mouths and raised eyebrows. This is an important step in the development of social skills.

Young children often mimic the emotions they see in other people. The urge to mimic the emotions of another person is called emotional contagion. No matter what age you are, when you see someone else smiling, you might find yourself beginning to smile.

[
This occurs because your brain perceives the smile on the other person's face and signals its own emotional circuits, triggering a smile on your face.
]

Neuroscientists believe that the human brain has mirror neurons that explain why we feel emotional empathy. It's thought that when you see the emotion of another person, a small number of mirror neurons in your brain begin to fire. These same neurons would activate if you were experiencing the emotion yourself. Mirror neurons might also be active when you learn language and imitate the movements of others.

EMOTIONS AND MEMORY

When you think about your life, do you better remember moments of emotion or the times you were bored? Most people remember the times of emotion. Emotions make it easier for the brain to create and retain memories.

BRAIN TEASER

Some secondary emotions, such as guilt, are learned through social conditioning and negative feedback.

AUTISM

Damage to mirror neurons has been linked to autism, a developmental disorder. This might explain why people with autism have difficulty empathizing with others, which can lead to impaired social skills and behavior.

Animals have mirror neurons, but they are probably not as developed as mirror neurons in humans.

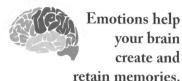

Emotions help your brain create and retain memories.

Simple memories that do not have emotions attached to them are encoded by the hippocampus. When emotion attaches to memory, the amygdala has an important role in processing it. Sensations that promote strong emotional responses stimulate the amygdala, which then communicates with the hypothalamus and triggers the release of hormones and other chemicals. The brain reacts by using many more neurons to encode the memory.

You might find it easy to remember all of the details of the day you first brought home your beloved family dog. These memories stay with you because they were encoded with powerful emotions.

FEAR, ANXIETY, AND ANGER

Has anyone ever said that you were being negative? The human brain is actually biased to be negative. You keep bad news and events in your memory longer than happy news. Unpleasant stimuli trigger the brain more powerfully than pleasant stimuli.

This negativity bias is another survival tool. Negative emotions such as fear, anxiety, and anger trigger a physical fight-or-flight response in the body, giving you the best chance of survival when facing danger.

In prehistoric times, the emotion of anger helped strong males fight for dominance. The winners survived to produce offspring, while the weaker males were less likely to survive and reproduce.

Today, humans still experience anger. You may have felt angry when defending a friend or protecting your possessions. Anger emotions release cortisol, which increases feelings of stress and frustration. Like fear, anger follows several pathways that begin with the limbic system.

THE POSITIVE SIDE OF EMOTIONS

Positive emotions, such as joy and happiness, motivate you to seek rewards. Pleasurable stimuli, such as watching your favorite baseball player hit a home run, activate brain areas close to the limbic system. Pleasure centers in your brain release neurotransmitters and endorphins, including dopamine, that make you feel good. Researchers have found that some areas of the brain near the limbic system, including the hypothalamus, are associated with happy emotions.

All animals, including humans, have reward systems in their brains. For many, the reward system is triggered by food or sex, which motivates them to eat and reproduce. These activities are essential for long-term survival of the species.

Sometimes, the brain's reward system can be affected by drugs or alcohol and become a part of an addiction to drugs. At first, these substances produce pleasure in the brain, just as natural rewards do. Over time and with increased use, the drug or alcohol is needed to stop unpleasant withdrawal symptoms, including nausea and shakiness.

YOUR BRAIN IN LOVE

What does it feel like to be in love? Does your heart race and your palms sweat?

Falling in love causes the brain to release feel-good neurotransmitters that trigger these physical reactions. When you fall in love, levels of several neurotransmitters, including dopamine, adrenaline, and norepinephrine, increase. Dopamine creates the feeling of euphoria that puts a smile on your face. Adrenaline and norepinephrine cause your heart to beat faster, your body to feel restless, and your skin to flush.

KEY QUESTIONS

- **Which parts of the brain are involved in processing emotions?**
- **Why are memories that have a lot of emotion associated with them easier to recall than memories that don't involve a lot of emotion?**
- **What role do mirror neurons play in our day-to-day lives and why is that important?**
- **What is the difference between mood and emotion?**

MIRRORING EMOTIONS

Does seeing someone cry make you feel sad? Empathy is the ability to identify with and understand another person's situation, feelings, or motives. Neuroscientists believe that the human brain has a system called mirror neurons that explain why we feel emotional empathy. In this experiment, you will investigate empathy and mirroring emotions.

Ideas for Supplies ▼

- 2 volunteers
- 2 chairs
- blindfold
- timer

- **Search the Internet for video clips of people expressing different emotions.** Try to find examples of happiness, sadness, anger, surprise, fear, and disgust. Are some emotions easier to find than others?

- **Divide yourselves into three groups: A, B, and C.** Have volunteer A sit at the computer and view one of the video clips while wearing headphones. The other volunteers shouldn't be able to see or hear the video.

- **At the same time, have volunteer B watch A as he or she watches the video clip.** B should be able to see A's face, but not see or hear the video clip A is watching. What does B notice? Have B write down what changes he or she observes on A's face and what emotions A's face matches.

- **At the same time, have volunteer C watch B's face.** C should write down the changes in B's facial expression, matching it with an emotion. C should not be able to see the video or A's facial expressions. What are the results? Did the emotions observed on A's face and B's face match?

- **Repeat the experiment using different video clips that show other emotions.** What are your results? Are the emotions viewed by the observers similar or different? Why or why not? Are some emotions recognized more easily than others?

> To investigate more, videotape volunteer A as he or she watches the emotion videos. Show your video to volunteers who were not in the room when volunteer A watched the emotion clips. Can they identify which emotions the viewer is watching? How? What facial movements are associated with different emotions?

VOCAB LAB 📖

Write down what you think each word means: **mood**, **fear response**, **adrenaline**, **mirror neurons**, **withdrawal**.

Discuss your definitions with friends using real-life examples. Did you all come up with the same definitions? Turn to the text and the glossary if you need help.

THEY WON'T LET ME PLAY WITH MY PHONE IN THE LAB! I'M TOTALLY HAVING WITHDRAWAL.

MY MIRROR NEURONS ARE NOT FIRING AT ALL.

FEAR RESPONSE

Fear prepares you for flight by sending adrenaline through your body to make your heart beat faster, your palms sweat, and your muscles contract. You'll need volunteers and a timer to test people's responses to fear stimuli in this experiment.

FIGHT-OR-FLIGHT

Fear, anger, frustration, and anxiety cause the body to produce an automatic fight-or-flight response. Whenever you sense a fear stimulus, the amygdala fires instant signals to the heart, lungs, and other body organs. Other nerves in the brain stem release chemicals that stimulate the heart and increase its rhythm.

- **Have your volunteers choose a scary thing to do.** Ideas include riding a bike down a steep hill or going on a roller coaster, but nothing dangerous. Volunteers should check and record their resting pulse rates.

- **Do the scary scenario.** Remind everyone to wear a helmet to protect their brains!

- **Have volunteers record their pulse rates immediately after the experience.** Record them again five minutes later. Ask each volunteer to rate the experience from 1 to 5, with 5 being the scariest. What conclusions can you come to?

To investigate more, repeat the experiment and measure other body changes that signal fear. Is there a connection between how the volunteers rated the experience and their body changes?

Chapter 5 ▶
Memory and Learning

How does the brain make memory and learning possible?

...AND MARK TEIXEIRA BATTED .292, AND THAT IS THE ENTIRE *2009* YANKEES ROSTER!

THAT WAS AMAZING!

HOLD ON JUST ONE SECOND...

HOW CAN YOU REMEMBER ALL THAT AND NOT REMEMBER THE FOUR LOBES OF THE BRAIN?

I GUESS MY BRAIN ONLY REMEMBERS THE IMPORTANT STUFF.

When you remember something, the neurons in your brain that were active during the original event are reactivated and fire again.

The first signs of memory occur in babies around the age of two to three months when they smile at familiar faces.

What did you have for dinner last night? Chicken, fish, spaghetti? What about three weeks ago? The content of your dinner plate from three weeks ago is probably a small, unimportant detail that has slipped your mind.

But what if that dinner was a birthday celebration for your 90-year-old grandfather? You might be able to recall the entire menu, along with what you were wearing and what music was playing. These details have been encoded in your brain as memories. How does your brain choose what information to store?

While most of the details of your day-to-day life are quickly forgotten, a few get encoded in your brain as memories. A memory is a reconstruction of a past event. When you remember an event, the same neurons in your brain that were active during the original event are reactivated and fire again. Remembering poetry, a childhood event, or recognizing a face are all parts of memory and involve a reconstruction of a past experience.

MEMORY SELECTION

Memory formation consists of several stages, from short-term memory to long-term memory. It can take up to two years to create a long-term memory. Once encoded, however, you might have that memory for the rest of your life. Long-term memories include important facts and information, as well as events and images from your past.

> If an experience registers strongly in your sensory cortex and hippocampus when it first happens, it is more likely to become a long-term memory.

At any given moment, the brain receives millions of bits of information from the senses. Sensory memory stores this incoming information only for an instant. Most of it remains unprocessed, while a few pieces of information transfer to short-term memory. Generally, short-term memory can hold information for only about 20 seconds. It also has a limited capacity. Only about seven pieces of information can be held at a time.

Some things you only have to remember for a short time. To order dinner, you look up the phone number of the local pizzeria and remember it just long enough to dial the phone. You're holding the phone number in your working memory.

Working memory is a type of short-term memory that holds sensations for a few seconds up to about 10 minutes while you process it. This allows the brain to work as efficiently as possible.

DON'T EAT THAT!

Human memory evolved as a survival tool. Early humans who were able to remember that a certain berry was poisonous could avoid eating that berry and have a better chance at survival. If the memory about the berry was stored with lots of other, unimportant details, it might have gotten lost. In order to be efficient, the brain retains and stores only those memories that are useful in some way.

Events that have emotional meaning for you, such as birthdays and getting your drivers' license, activate more neurons in your brain than insignificant events.

A "flashbulb" memory occurs when extremely vivid, emotional events occur. Many people have a very clear flashbulb memory of where they were and what they were doing when they heard about the terrorist attacks on September 11, 2001. Do you have a flashbulb memory of an important event that occurred during your lifetime?

SORRY. I CAN'T TAKE THE PICTURE. THE BATTERY'S DEAD.

THAT'S OKAY. I ALREADY TOOK A FLASHBULB MEMORY.

Think of your working memory as the surface of your desk. You store pieces of information there that you need to perform a specific task. If your desk gets too cluttered, you won't be able to work efficiently. When you are done with a task, clearing the desk for the next task will help you work most efficiently.

LONG-TERM MEMORY

Some experiences are stored in memory for days, months, and even years. Long-term memory includes memories of recent facts and events and older events and information. Long-term memory consists of four processes—encoding, consolidation, storage, and retrieval. These processes allow you to make a memory and recall that information later.

Experiences that cause long or intense neural activity in the brain are more likely to be encoded as long-term memories. These memories travel from working memory to the hippocampus, where they undergo further processing. Located in the forebrain, the hippocampus receives sensory data from the senses.

> The hippocampus encodes new memories and helps to recall others, turning short-term memories into long-term ones.

Memories can be encoded by repetition, a strategy you might use to learn your spelling words. Other times information is analyzed so that it has meaning and is linked to information already in long-term storage. You can make long-term memories by writing an essay about a particular subject.

A third way to encode memories for long-term storage involves a strong emotional reaction. If the amygdala is activated during the original experience, the memory will be linked to the emotional response.

When encoding, the brain assigns a meaning to the information. For example, your brain might encode the word apple as "fruit, round, red." If you could not remember the word apple immediately, then one of the words you used to encode it, such as "fruit," should help retrieve it.

CONSOLIDATION

After a memory is encoded, it is consolidated, making it more likely to stick around for a while. Consolidation uses a process called long-term potentiation. When the same neurons fire together frequently, they can become permanently sensitized to each other. These neurons are now more likely to fire together again in the future. This is called consolidation.

> The better a memory is consolidated, the more likely it is to last in long-term memory.

If you practice a piano piece over and over, neurons in your brain fire in a certain order. The more you play, the easier it is for your brain to repeat this pattern of firing and the better you become at playing the piece. In the same way, when a neural network is used over and over again, messages are more likely to flow along this familiar path.

PAY ATTENTION

When you focus your attention on an event or fact, you make it easier for your brain to create a memory. Attention intensifies your original experience. Focusing your attention on an event causes the neurons of your brain to fire more frequently. The more a neuron fires, the stronger its connections are with other brain cells. This makes the experience more intense and increases the chances that it will be encoded as a memory.

BRAIN TEASER

An event that triggered intense fear will activate the amygdala and result in a strongly encoded memory.

If a part of the brain is damaged and one part of a memory is lost, many other pieces of the memory remain. A stroke or other brain trauma may affect part of a memory, but rarely wipes it away entirely.

AMNESIA

When someone has excessive memory loss, they may be experiencing amnesia. This can be triggered by a physical injury to the brain or a psychological trauma. It can affect some areas of memory, but leave other areas in place. A person with amnesia may lose memories of the past year, but still retain memories from 20 years ago. Memories of personal experiences are typically affected the most severely. Many people with amnesia gradually recover their lost memories over time.

MEMORY STORAGE

Do you think of memory as a filing cabinet? Do you imagine that when you want to remember something, you find that particular file and take a look? The reality is much different!

Remember, when you experience a memory, you are actually experiencing the event all over again, not watching a recording or reading a file. Memories are not stored in any one place in the brain. Instead, they are stored as groups of neurons throughout the brain. These neuron groups are ready to fire together in the same pattern that they fired during the original experience.

Each component of a memory—the sights, sounds, smells, and emotions—are stored in the area of the brain that originally processed it. For example, groups of neurons in the visual cortex encode the sight of your favorite dog, while the auditory cortex stores the sound of his bark, and the amygdala stores the emotion attached to your dog. When you remember your dog, all of these neurons fire simultaneously to reconstruct your memory.

What happens if your auditory cortex is damaged? You might not be able to remember the sound of your dog's bark. But if your visual cortex is unharmed, you'll still be able to remember what your dog looks like.

[Storing the different pieces of a memory in different brain regions protects the memory.]

RECALLING A MEMORY

When we remember something, it is as if we are re-experiencing it all over again. It's like putting together a jigsaw puzzle. The pieces come from many different storage areas in the brain to form a complete picture or memory.

This reconstruction, however, is never exactly the same as the original experience. The pieces of memory can get mixed up, like puzzle pieces. When the brain retrieves a memory, it often mixes other information linked to the memory into the reconstruction. New information from the present day might get mixed into the memory, too. Some of the new associations stick to the original memory and get stored with it. The act of retrieving a memory can change it.

Recall an event that happened two or three years ago. Things you've heard or seen today could become mixed up with the memory. Next year, when you remember the event again, it might be slightly different than it is today. Your recall of past memories is often unreliable!

EXPLICIT VS. IMPLICIT MEMORY

Long-term memory can be divided into two categories: explicit memory and implicit memory. Explicit memories are expressed with words. One kind of explicit memory reconstructs your personal past experiences and includes sensations and emotions. It's called an episodic memory because it often feels like a movie from your own point of view. An episodic memory activates the brain's areas that were fired during the original experience. Remembering your 10th birthday party is an example of episodic memory.

...AND THEN ANAKIN AND KATNISS GET ON THEIR BROOMS AND FLY TO HOGWARTS!

YOU'VE GOT SOME SERIOUSLY MIXED UP MEMORY JIGSAW PUZZLE PIECES!

MOUSE MEMORIES

Researchers have used advanced imaging techniques to record how memories are made in a mouse's brain. You can watch the neurons being activated during memory making in this short video.

I HAVEN'T EVEN TASTED THIS SANDWICH YET, BUT I ALREADY LIKE IT!

SUBJECT DISPLAYS EXCELLENT FOOD-BASED IMPLICIT MEMORY.

Have you ever had the spooky sense that you've experienced the current moment in the past? This phenomenon is called déjà vu. The word *déjà vu* is a French word that means "already seen."

Another kind of explicit memory is a semantic memory, which stores your knowledge of the world. It includes facts, rules, ideas, and concepts, but does not have a personal connection. Semantic memory helps you remember facts for the upcoming social studies test.

Implicit memories are expressed in ways other than words. Some implicit memories are procedural memories that are related to actions, such as walking, swimming, or riding a bike. Procedural memories are unconscious. They enable you to carry out ordinary motor actions without thinking about it.

Other implicit memories are conditioned emotional responses. Have you ever not liked someone from the first moment you met him or her but didn't know why? It's probably because you have an implicit memory of a similar person whom you dislike.

WHEN MEMORY FAILS

You forget things every day. Forgetting can be caused by a failure at any point in the memory process—an encoding mistake, a storage error, or problems with retrieval.

How information is encoded into memory affects your ability to remember it. Information processed at deeper levels with more associations is harder to forget. Do you study for a test while watching television? If the information is not encoded properly because you're distracted by the television, it's more likely to be forgotten and you'll do worse on your test.

Some memories fade over time, especially those in sensory and short-term memory. Other memories are forgotten because other information interferes with them. People can also experience memory loss as a result of a physical injury or trauma.

Have you ever felt like someone's name was on the tip of your tongue but you just couldn't remember it? This type of forgetting is probably caused by a retrieval failure. Context clues can sometimes help you remember. That's why people say to retrace your steps when you're trying to remember something.

[Should you be worried about forgetting? No! Forgetting is a necessary process.]

Remember that clean desktop? If your brain wasn't able to forget things it would be overwhelmed with information that it no longer needs.

LEARNING

Memory and learning are closely connected. Learning is when you gain new information about the world, and memory stores that information. Memory is a record of the learning process.

In the brain, learning occurs when the brain's structure changes in response to new experiences. Neurons make new connections or change existing connections. Learning depends on memory to store and retrieve the information learned. When new knowledge is stored in memory, it is often linked to existing knowledge by association. Learning and memory make you who you are.

Learning new things requires plasticity of the brain, or the ability to change in response to experience. Neuroscientists believe that with repeated stimuli, neurons physically change the number of neurotransmitters released and the sensitivity of receptor sites across the synapses.

DÉJÀ VU

Déjà vu might occur when a new experience recalls the memory of a similar experience in the past. As the memory is recalled, it's confused with the present experience. This creates a sense of recognition without bringing the past event to mind. Déjà vu might occur when a new experience is incorrectly marked as familiar when processed in the limbic system.

KEY QUESTIONS

- What are the different stages of memory?

- What are the processes of long-term memory?

- What is the difference between explicit and implicit memory? Which one are you using when you think about your friend's party?

TEST YOUR WORKING MEMORY

Most people can only hold about seven pieces of information in working memory. Some can hold a little more. Others can hold a little less. What about you?

* pencil and paper
* list of numbers (see below)
  * 593
  * 6371
  * 63692
  * 398104
  * 5729381
  * 36190528
  * 479271036
  * 8341690237

* **Begin at the top of the number list.** Look at the first number and try to memorize it. Cover the number with your hand. From memory, try to write the number on a piece of paper without pausing.

* **Move on to the next number on the list and repeat the same process.** Continue down the list, memorizing each number. At what point do you have trouble remembering the entire number? How do you explain your results?

> To investigate more, repeat the experiment using strings of random letters or shapes. Does this affect your results? Try repeating the activity with several friends. How do their results compare to each other and to you? What conclusion can you make about the results?

WELL, YOU REMEMBERED FIVE NUMBERS THIS TIME.

WHY DO I NEED TO REMEMBER NUMBERS WHEN MY PHONE DOES IT FOR ME?

WHAT IF YOU LOST YOUR PHONE AND NEEDED TO REMEMBER A NUMBER TO CALL?

HOW DO YOU CALL SOMEONE IF YOU LOSE YOUR PHONE?

CREATE A FALSE MEMORY

Is it possible to remember something that never really happened? Memory is not perfect. Sometimes, your brain makes mistakes. In this activity, you will investigate how the brain can create a false memory.

Ideas for Supplies ▼

- paper and pencils
- several volunteers
- timer

- **Create a list of 14 words all related to a central theme.** A school-themed list might include the following words: read, pages, letters, numbers, school, study, scores, test, pen, pencil, paper, words, teacher, classroom.

- **Make a second list of 14 random words.** Include two words from your first list on the second list. Make one of the words on the second list fit the theme of the first list, but this word should not be one that was actually included in the first list. For example, the second list could include the words "letters" and "study" from the first list and a new word, "book."

- **Show the first list to your volunteers and ask them to remember the words.** Wait about five minutes and then show the volunteers the second list. Ask them which words on the second list they remember from the first list.

- **How many volunteers identified the related word that was not on the first list?** What results did you find? How do you explain your results?

To investigate more, consider how the amount of time the volunteers study the first list affects your results. Repeat the activity using different word lists or different volunteers. Give some volunteers a shorter time to study the first list, and give a second group a longer time to study the same list. What do you observe? Why do you think this happens?

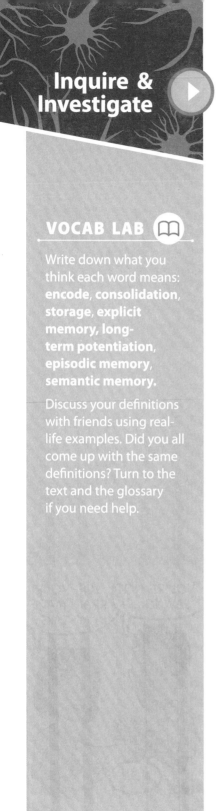

VOCAB LAB

Write down what you think each word means: **encode, consolidation, storage, explicit memory, long-term potentiation, episodic memory, semantic memory.**

Discuss your definitions with friends using real-life examples. Did you all come up with the same definitions? Turn to the text and the glossary if you need help.

CHUNKING TO REMEMBER

If the average human brain can only hold about seven pieces of information in short-term memory at a time, how do we manage when we need to remember more? Chunking is a technique used to increase how much information can be retained in short-term memory. Chunking combines small pieces of information into larger, more familiar pieces.

In this activity, you will work with a partner to investigate how chunking increases short-term memory capacity.

- **Write down a four-word phrase, then rewrite it on a separate piece of paper divided up into two-letter pairs.** Show the letter pairs to a partner. Ten seconds later, can your partner write the letters down from memory without looking? Most people will have trouble remembering the letters 10 seconds later because their short-term memories can't handle that amount of information.

PLANES TRAINS AND AUTOMOBILES

PL AN ES TR AI NS AN DA UT OM OB IL ES

- **What if the information is chunked into the larger, familiar words?** If you show the first piece of paper, can your partner write the letters down 10 seconds later? Presented this way the information is much easier to remember because short-term memory can easily hold four pieces of information.

- **Now read the numbers 1 to 15 in random order to your partner at a rate of about one per second.** When you are finished reading the numbers, your partner should immediately write down the numbers he or she remembers.

- **Now read the numbers 1 to 15 in order to your partner at the same rate of about one per second.** When you are finished, your partner should immediately write down the numbers he or she remembers.

- **How do the results compare between the first series and the second series of numbers?** How do you explain your results?

To investigate more, use another way to chunk information by finding a pattern in the data you want to remember. For example, the numbers 1, 4, 7, 10, 13, 16, 19 are easy to remember because each number increases by three. Design a new chunking test using patterns to group the information. How does this chunking technique improve short-term memory?

Ideas for Supplies ▼

- pencil and paper
- several volunteers
- timer

CREATE A MNEMONIC

What can help you memorize a long list of words for a test? Memory techniques called mnemonics can help. A mnemonic uses rhymes, acronyms, diagrams, and other methods to help you remember information such as dates, facts, and words.

One example of a mnemonic is the acronym HOMES, which stands for the names of the five Great Lakes—Huron, Ontario, Michigan, Erie, and Superior. Another mnemonic technique turns the first letter of each word in a list into a sentence. For example, to remember the six noble gases from the periodic table for your chemistry test—helium, neon, argon, radon, krypton, and xenon—you could create the following sentence: Harry Napped After Rapidly Kicking a Xylophone.

In this activity, you'll create your own mnemonic and test how well it works. You can use whatever you want to create the mnemonic: words, music, names, shapes, spellings, or images.

- **Make a list of at least eight words.** You can pick anything you like. Develop a mnemonic to help others remember the list of words.

- **Split your volunteers into two groups.** Give the first group the list of words but do not give them the mnemonic. Ask them to study the list for five minutes.

- **After one hour, test each member of the first group by having them write the words from the list on a blank piece of paper.** They cannot help each other. Time how long it takes them to remember the list of words. Record your results. Review their papers and record the accuracy.

- **Repeat the procedure with the second group of volunteers, but give them the mnemonic to help them remember the list of words.** Allow them to study the list for five minutes and then test their memory after one hour has elapsed. Record your results.

- **Compare the results from the two groups.** What was different between the results of the first group and the second group? How do you explain the results? Did the mnemonic work?

> To investigate more, create a different mnemonic for the same list of words. For example, if you created a sentence using the first letter of each word, try thinking of an image that incorporates the words from the list. Repeat the experiment on a third group of volunteers using the new mnemonic. How do the results from this group compare to results from the first and second groups?

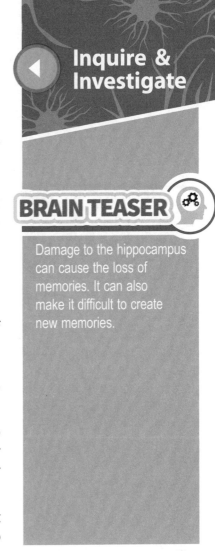

BRAIN TEASER

Damage to the hippocampus can cause the loss of memories. It can also make it difficult to create new memories.

MOST NOTABLY, EVERY MONKEY OPTS NOT TO IMBIBE CHEESE.

WHAT THE...?

IT'S MY MNEMONIC TO REMEMBER HOW TO SPELL MNEMONIC!

Ideas for Supplies

- mp3 player and headphones
- computer with Internet access
- timer
- paper and pencil
- several volunteers

PLAYERS GONNA PLAY PLAY PLAY PLAY PLAY!!!

I DON'T THINK LISTENING TO MUSIC IS GOING TO HELP HER SCORE

MUSIC AND MEMORY

How does music affect your memory? Do you prefer to study with or without music? Some people say that music helps them study. Others believe that it is distracting and hurts concentration.

In this experiment, you will test how listening to music affects your ability to concentrate on a task and complete the task.

- **Go to this link to play an online memory concentration game.** Play the game a few times to get used to how it works.

- **Listen to a song of your choice while you play the game again.** Record the time it takes you to complete the game. Now play the game again, with no music. Record your results.

- **Repeat the experiment with each volunteer, recording the results.** Let your volunteers choose their own music. Compare the results. Was there a difference in the amount of time it took to complete each game? What conclusions can you make?

> To investigate more, repeat the experiment but this time, instead of letting the volunteers play a song of their choice, choose a song for them. Does this affect the results? Analyze your results for other patterns. Do age or gender affect the results? How?

Chapter 6 ▶
Language and Speech

How does the brain make it possible for people to communicate?

The brain processes language primarily in Broca's area and Wernicke's area.

How do you know if your dog is happy, sad, excited, or angry? How does he hold his tail, ears, and mouth? Many animals communicate through body language. They use posture and gestures to convey how they feel and what they are thinking.

Humans also communicate with body language. Have you ever walked into a room where your parents are having a conversation and known they were talking about you? Can you tell just by looking at someone that he or she is friendly or wants to be left alone? We communicate thoughts, feelings, and intentions with body language and gestures. Body language makes up as much as 50 to 70 percent of our overall communication!

What makes us different from animals, however, is language. Only the human brain has specific areas dedicated to language. These parts of the brain enable us to speak, read, and write.

LANGUAGE AND THE BRAIN

Language is more than a bunch of letters or symbols put together. Language follows a set of complex rules. These rules change from language to language, but most of them share a similar level of complexity.

Language processing occurs primarily in two areas of the brain—Broca's area and Wernicke's area. For most people, these two areas are located in the left hemisphere of the brain. Broca's area and Wernicke's area are connected by a band of nerve fibers called the arcuate fasciculus.

Broca's area was named after Paul Broca, a French neurosurgeon who discovered that lesions in this area of the brain interfered with speech. Wernicke's area was named after a German neurologist.

[Together, these parts of the brain allow you to understand and speak language.]

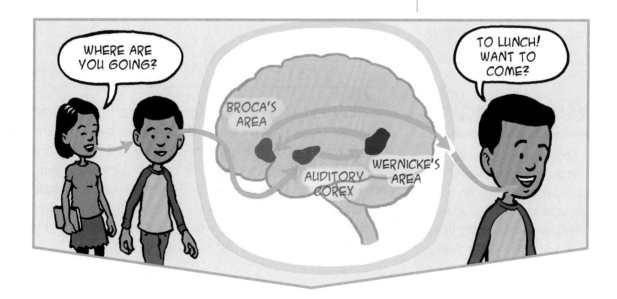

Wernicke's area is located in the upper temporal lobe. Generally, word comprehension occurs in Wernicke's area. When a person hears a word, Wernicke's area matches the sound to its meaning. Damage to Wernicke's area in the brain can cause difficulty understanding written and spoken language.

Broca's area is active in speaking language. When you want to say something, Wernicke's area finds the right words to match your thought. Then the words pass through the arcuate fasciculus to Broca's area, which turns the words into speech by sending signals to move your tongue, mouth, jaw, and larynx.

While scientists have learned much about how the brain processes language, there is still a lot to learn. Brain scans have shown large areas of the cortex near Wernicke's and Broca's areas that become active during language tasks. Scientists are working to understand the role of these areas in language processing.

[
Wernicke's area helps you choose the right word, while Broca's area helps you say the word.
]

LISTENING AND SPEAKING

Listening and speaking are some of the brain's most complex jobs. The process of listening begins with sound. When you hear your friend say, "Hey, how are you?" the sound of his voice is received by your ears and sent to the auditory cortex. From there, the signals are sent to receptive language areas of the brain that decode words. Other areas in the brain evaluate the emotion, tone, and rhythm of the speech.

Within a few milliseconds, the amygdala assesses the emotional tone of the speech and produces an appropriate emotional reaction. In this case, your emotions are probably happy, because you are talking to your buddy. If your brain senses that the tone of the speech is threatening, the amygdala might trigger a fight-or-flight fear response.

Wernicke's area processes the structure of the words, while other parts of the brain start to process the meaning of the words. In the frontal lobe, the words are associated with memories, which enables you to retrieve the meaning of the word. This is a lot of brain activity packed into about a half second of time.

When you want to respond to your friend's conversation, your brain has to find the right words to express your thoughts. First, your brain forms concepts and ideas. Then, in the temporal lobe, the brain retrieves words from memory and matches them to the concepts. These words are turned into sounds in Wernicke's area. This information travels to Broca's area to match the word sounds to the mouth, tongue, and throat movement needed for speech.

LATERALIZATION AND LANGUAGE

Although the human brain is divided into two hemispheres, not all of the paired structures are completely identical. This difference is called brain lateralization. A lateralized function is one that is controlled more by one side of the brain. The side that exerts more control is dominant. For the vast majority of right-handed people, language processing occurs in the left hemisphere. Many left-handed people also process language in the left hemisphere. Some use their right hemispheres, while a few process language equally in both hemispheres.

Finally, Broca's area sends signals to the motor cortex to move the mouth, tongue, and throat in order to speak the words. You answer your friend with, "Hey, I'm fine. How are you?"

In most people, the left hemisphere interprets the literal meaning of the words, while the right hemisphere processes the emotional meaning of the words. If your friend says, "You look great," he might mean very different things depending on how he speaks. Was he enthusiastic or sarcastic? It takes both sides of your brain to listen to people accurately.

READING AND WRITING

While you are born with an innate ability for language and speech, learning how to read and write is a whole different story. Reading uses several areas of the brain that work together to link the sound, spelling, and meaning of a word.

To learn reading and writing, you first have to decode the shapes of written letters and turn them into the sounds they would make if you were to speak them aloud. To do this, the visual cortex processes the shapes of the written letters and words. It sends this information to the language areas of the brain, including Wernicke's area.

The auditory cortex allows a reader to recognize each word by the way it sounds. Once a word has been recognized, Broca's area links the written word to the spoken word. The temporal lobe matches the words to their meanings.

Writing is even more complex. In addition to using visual areas of the brain to decode text and language areas to understand words, writing also activates brain areas that control hand movement and manual dexterity.

BRAIN TEASER

Brain-imaging techniques such as PET scans and functional MRIs allow scientists to study human communication and the brain.

Writing by hand can help your brain learn and remember. Studies have found that children and adults who write new characters by hand are better able to recognize and remember the characters later. Other studies have found that finger movements used in hand writing can activate the brain regions used in thinking, language, and working memory.

> In one study, children in second, fourth, and sixth grades were able to write more words faster—and expressed more ideas—when they wrote essays by hand instead of with a computer keyboard.

Scientists believe handwriting may help you learn because it more actively engages your brain. When you write something down, you stimulate a group of cells in the base of your brain known as the reticular activating system (RAS). The RAS filters all of the information your brain processes. It focuses more of your attention on what you are currently working on. The physical act of writing triggers the RAS, which sends a signal to the cerebral cortex to pay attention.

KEY QUESTIONS

- What areas of the brain are involved in language and communication?

- How are language and memory connected in the brain? If the parts of your brain that handle memory are damaged, will you be able to communicate verbally with other people? Why or why not?

- Why is writing more complex than listening and speaking?

LEARNING DISABILITIES

Some kids in your classroom may get extra help from a teacher because of a learning disability. Learning disabilities can occur at any point in the language processing process. People with an auditory processing disorder have trouble telling the difference between sounds. Those with a visual processing disorder may have problems reading, interpreting maps, or other visual tasks. Dysgraphia is a disorder in the writing process that may cause problems with handwriting, spelling, and idea organization. Dyslexia is a group of language-processing disorders that can interfere with reading. Luckily, there are now many treatments for learning disabilities, so most people can get the help they need to be academically successful.

Ideas for Supplies ▼

- several colored markers
- pencil
- pen
- ruler
- package of 3-by-5-inch note cards
- timer
- volunteer

THE STROOP EFFECT

What happens when the brain receives two conflicting signals? You can investigate with a simple activity based on the Stroop effect. In the 1930s, J. Ridley Stroop discovered that when the word "red" was printed in a different color, it was more difficult for the person to say the color. Stroop concluded that two conflicting signals—the word and the color—created interference and caused a problem in the brain's processing.

The anterior cingulate is the area of the brain that processes these signals. One theory to explain the Stroop effect is that the interference occurs when the words are read faster than the colors are named in the brain. Another theory is that interference occurs because naming colors takes more of the brain's attention than reading words.

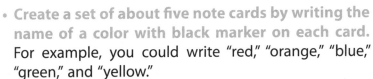
- Create a set of about five note cards by writing the name of a color with black marker on each card. For example, you could write "red," "orange," "blue," "green," and "yellow."

- Create a second set of note cards by writing the same color words. This time, use a colored marker that does not match the word's color meaning. For example, write the word "red" using a blue marker and the word "yellow" using a purple marker.

- Say the word on each of the cards in the first set as fast as you can. Have a volunteer time you.

- Now say the word on each of the cards in the second set as fast as you can. Have a volunteer time you. Was there a difference between the two sets?

- Go through the second set again, but this time say the color used to write the words. For example if the word "blue" is written in red marker, you will say "red." Have a volunteer time you. How did your results compare to the first and second times?

- Repeat the activity by having the volunteer read while you operate the timer. How do the results compare?

To investigate more, repeat the experiment using a larger group of volunteers. Group your volunteers according to age or gender. What are your results? What conclusions can you make?

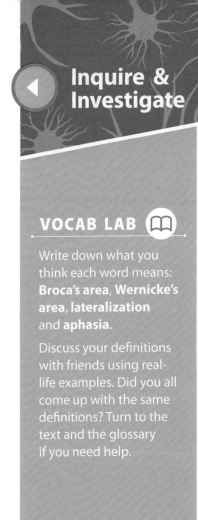

VOCAB LAB 📖

Write down what you think each word means: **Broca's area**, **Wernicke's area**, **lateralization** and **aphasia**.

Discuss your definitions with friends using real-life examples. Did you all come up with the same definitions? Turn to the text and the glossary if you need help.

Ideas for Supplies ▼

- video camera
- a few volunteers to act in video clips
- computer or tablet
- volunteers to watch the video clips and answer a few questions

INTERPRETING BODY LANGUAGE

You can speak volumes without saying a word. How? Through body language! When you look at someone, your brain receives visual input about that person's mood, emotions, and intent. In this activity, you will test how well different people perceive and interpret subtle body language clues.

- **Think of a few examples of body language to explore in your video.** Do you want your actors to show happiness, excitement, disapproval, or anger? Can you think of some other emotions for your actors to use?

- **Think of scenarios for your actors to play out with no dialogue.** Rehearse these scenes with your actors a few times. Film your volunteer actors as they act out your examples.

- **Ask a second group of volunteers to watch the video.** Have them write down what emotions they perceive based on the body language of the actors in the video. How did the perceived emotions compare to the actual emotions being portrayed by the actors? Were they the same? Different? How do you explain your results? Analyze your results by gender and age. Did one group perform better than another? Why or why not?

BRAIN TEASER

The Pirahã tribe in the Amazon have no words for colors. Instead, they describe colors using phrases that can change with each use. If you show them a red cup, they might say, "This looks like blood."

> To investigate more, add dialogue to your scenarios and re-film, using the same body language. Does the addition of words affect how your volunteers interpret the body language?

Chapter 7 ▶
The Healthy Brain

What can you do to keep your brain healthy?

Environmental factors such as sleep, diet, and exercise can affect how your brain works.

Have you ever had a day when you didn't get enough sleep the night before? What if you then ate an unhealthy breakfast before spending the day sitting in a classroom? How did you feel? Did your brain work well for you?

Keeping your brain healthy is a top priority! Lots of environmental factors, including the sleep you get each night, the food you put in your body, and how much you exercise, affect how well your brain works.

BRAIN FOOD

Did you know that what you eat affects your brain? A balanced diet has the potential to protect the brain and reduce the chance of developing certain mental disorders. Scientists continue to study the link between food and the brain to see if changes in diet can improve cognitive ability, protect the brain from damage, and slow the aging process.

Some foods have already been linked to healthy brains. Foods that are high in omega-3 fatty acids, such as salmon, walnuts, and kiwi fruit, improve brain health. Omega-3 fatty acids improve learning and memory processes. These fatty acids also fight against mental disorders such as depression, schizophrenia, and dementia.

Researchers have found that children who have increased amounts of omega-3 fatty acids in their diet perform better in school with reading and spelling tasks. They also display fewer behavioral problems. In contrast, people who eat a diet that includes little omega-3 fatty acids have an increased risk of several mental disorders, such as attention deficit disorder, dyslexia, dementia, depression, bipolar disorder, and schizophrenia.

Folic acid, found in spinach, orange juice, and yeast, is essential for healthy brain function. Low levels of folic acid can lead to disorders such as depression and other cognitive impairment.

> A healthy amount of folic acid in the diet has been shown to prevent cognitive decline and dementia as the brain ages.

The people of India, where there is a low occurrence of Alzheimer's disease, include a spice in their diet that might protect the brain from the disease. In tests, the curry spice curcumin has been shown to reduce memory problems in animal models of Alzheimer's disease and brain trauma. Curcumin is found in the spice turmeric.

LIVE LONG AND PROSPER

Research has found that eating a healthy diet can help your brain's cells by strengthening neural synapses and providing other benefits to cognitive processes. Need some proof? Look no further than Okinawa, an island in Japan. Residents of Okinawa frequently eat fish high in omega-3 fatty acids. They also exercise regularly. The residents have one of the world's longest lifespans, 78 years for men and 86 years for women, along with a very low rate of mental disorders.

Omega-3 fatty acids support brain plasticity and the expression of molecules related to learning and memory. Foods rich in omega-3 fatty acids include trout, sardines, eggs, milk, walnuts, flaxseed, peanut butter, Brussels sprouts, and certain oils.

Antioxidants, which are found in blueberries, kale, coffee, and nuts, can also protect the brain. The human body naturally produces negatively charged oxygen compounds as part of metabolism. These compounds can trigger chemical chain reactions that damage or kill cells. The brain is particularly vulnerable because of its high level of neuron activity. A diet high in antioxidants can prevent the chemical chain reactions and cell damage from occurring.

While some foods can help your brain, others have the opposite effect. Diets high in trans fats and saturated fats negatively affect the brain. Researchers have found that eating junk food and fast food negatively affects the brain's synapses, particularly in areas related to learning and memory.

[What's on your dinner plate? Is it food that will help or hurt your brain?]

EXERCISE

It might seem strange to think that going for a jog will improve your math grade, but it's true! With a healthy diet, regular exercise can improve brain function, from learning math to improving your memory.

Throughout your life, exercise enhances the growth and survival of new neurons in the hippocampus, a critical area for long-term memory and learning. These new neurons may be able to replace others that degenerate due to aging or disease. Exercise can increase brain alertness and lead to faster learning.

Some of the cognitive benefits of exercise may be caused by an increase in blood that flows to the brain.

The greater the blood flow, the faster oxygen and other important nutrients reach the brain's neurons.

> Researchers have found that physical exercise can improve brain function throughout your entire life–it's never too late to help your brain with exercise!

SLEEP

When you go to sleep, your brain does not turn off like the lights in a room. Sleep occurs in cycles, and your brain goes through different levels of activity during each cycle. Stage 1 is light sleep, where you can be easily woken. In stage 2, brain wave activity slows down. Deep sleep occurs in stages 3 and 4, when brain activity is low. In the fifth state, which is rapid eye movement (REM) sleep, your brain's activity increases to a level similar to a brain that is awake. Your most vivid dreams occur during REM sleep. After REM sleep, you return to stage 1 and repeat the cycle. The longer you sleep, the longer your REM stages become, while the deeper sleep of stages 3 and 4 shortens.

How much sleep you need varies by age, health, and individual sleep patterns. Infants and children need more sleep than adult men and women. Most teens need about nine hours of sleep, while adults function best on seven to eight hours.

Scientists are working to understand why the brain needs sleep. One theory is that the brain needs downtime from the sensory input of the outside world in order to sort, process, and memorize information. Important memory functions occur during sleep.

A LIFETIME OF SLEEP

About one-third of your life is spent sleeping. If you live to be 75 years old, you will have slept for 25 years! Sleep is an important part of brain and body health. You can watch the areas of the brain that are active during sleep.

JUST ONE MORE LEVEL! I'LL FINISH MY PROJECT TOMORROW.

THE ADDICT CONTINUES TO DISPLAY IMPAIRED JUDGMENT.

The hippocampus collects, sorts, and sends messages about information gathered by the senses. Some of that information is put into long-term memory storage in different areas of the brain. Many scientists believe that sleep has a role in the process, allowing the brain to consolidate memories.

DRUGS AND ALCOHOL

Some substances, such as drugs and alcohol, can change brain function. These mind-altering substances affect the way neurotransmitters function. Some mimic brain neurotransmitters, while others block neurotransmitters from working properly.

Some drugs are addictive. They have a powerful influence on the brain's neural networks that are linked to rewards. When users take an addictive drug, the brain creates feelings of well-being, euphoria, and calm. For example, cocaine releases the neurotransmitter dopamine in the brain's nucleus accumbens, an area linked to pleasurable sensation. Nicotine, a very addictive drug found in tobacco, also activates dopamine in the brain.

> If you start smoking regularly, it's very difficult to stop, even when you know about the disastrous health effects of smoking, which include cancer and heart disease.

Drug and alcohol use can also cause physical changes in the brain. Scans of drug addicts' brains show lower levels of activity in the prefrontal cortex. In lab animal studies, long-term use of addictive drugs lowers the activity of neural networks in the cortex that links with the nucleus accumbens. This influences response inhibition and plan formation. It may explain why many drug addicts exhibit impaired judgment and, because of their addiction, lose their jobs, homes, and families.

DISEASES AND DISORDERS

As we've seen, the brain is an incredibly complicated organ. Sometimes, something can go wrong.

Accident, stroke, trauma, infection—physical damage from any of these scenarios can result in a brain disorder and cause a person to lose certain brain functions. Because the brain controls the body and the mind, damage to the brain can mean arms and legs fail to work properly, or emotions and moods are adversely affected, or language is interrupted.

Developmental disorders occur when something goes wrong in the growing brain. Brain development is a very sensitive process. Any environmental stress, such as oxygen deprivation before or during birth, hunger, or even extreme emotional stress can cause permanent brain damage.

We hear about post-traumatic stress disorder in the news a lot these days. PTSD is a mental health condition triggered by a terrifying event, such as a war, accident, or attack.

SHOULD I EVEN ASK ABOUT THE HELMET?

I'VE GOT A BIG TEST TOMORROW. GOTTA PROTECT MY HEAD!

DARNIT! COULD I BORROW YOUR HELMET?

WHY? WHAT'S UP?

I DROPPED MY PENCIL AND I ALWAYS HIT MY HEAD UNDER THE TABLE.

Have you ever known an elderly person who repeats himself, is unable to respond to questions, or who forgets how to work simple tools such as the microwave? They may be suffering from a degenerative condition such as Alzheimer's disease.

> Brain function can be disturbed by degeneration from illness or aging, resulting in memory loss, cognitive impairment, and dementia.

Do you know anyone who has had a concussion? You may have even had one yourself. A concussion occurs when you get a blow to the head or hit something very hard. The brain shifts and hits the inside of your skull's bone. If this happens with a lot of force, the brain can be bruised and damaged. A concussion occurs if the brain experiences a temporary change in the way it works after being bumped or jarred. Most concussions are caused by car crashes, playground accidents, or sports collisions.

Some concussions last a short time. Other concussions can last for days or even weeks. Severe concussions are medical emergencies that should be treated in a hospital emergency department. Most of the time, people return to normal activity after a concussion. Someone who has suffered repeated concussions, however, may develop long-lasting problems with movement, learning, or speaking.

The best way to prevent a concussion is to protect your head. Always wear a seatbelt in a car. Wear a helmet, headgear, and other safety equipment when you are riding a bike, skateboarding, riding a scooter, playing contact sports, or participating in other activities with a risk of hitting your head.

MUCH MORE TO LEARN

For thousands of years, humans have studied the brain and its role in our thoughts, feelings, memories, and every part of our lives. In recent years, scientists have learned more about the human brain than ever before. There have been amazing advances in the treatment of brain diseases and disorders, discoveries about brain function, and new technologies for studying how the brain works.

Yet the more we learn about the brain, the more we realize how much more there is to learn. So much about the human brain remains a mystery, and the study of this complex organ is ongoing. Every day, scientists are working to understand more about the brain and how it works.

> No one can predict where brain science will lead or what it will look like in the future.

It is possible that the brain may be so complicated that we may never fully understand all of its inner workings. However, the journey of investigating and discovering new things about the human brain is certain to be a thrilling ride.

HEADACHES

The brain itself does not have pain nerve receptors. So why do you get a headache? The most common type of headache, the tension headache, is probably caused by tension in the meninges, the blood vessels, or the muscles of the head and neck. This tension stimulates pain receptors, which send signals to the brain's sensory cortex. Bam! You have a headache. Other headaches, such as migraines, are thought to be caused by an over-activity of neurons, affecting the brain's sensory cortex.

KEY QUESTIONS

- **How do exercise, sleep, and diet affect brain function?**

- **What are the stages of sleep? What happens in each stage?**

- **Why is it important to know the effects of drugs and alcohol on the brain and on the body?**

PROTECTING THE BRAIN

Every year, more than 400,000 kids go to the hospital emergency room for a brain injury or concussion. Wearing a helmet during physical activities such as bike riding or hockey can help to protect your brain from injury.

In this activity, you will investigate how a helmet protects the brain by designing a protective helmet for an "egg" head. Try this activity outside, since it can be pretty messy!

- **Spread the newspaper on the ground.** Drop the egg from about shoulder height onto the newspaper. What happens? Clean up and replace the newspaper.

- **How can you protect an egg being dropped from shoulder height so it doesn't break?** Using your imagination, create a design and build a helmet for another egg.

- **Drop the egg from the same height onto the newspaper.** What happens? If your egg breaks again, go back to the drawing board and design a new helmet.

- **Try out several different helmet designs.** Which designs protect the egg and which do not? Why do you think this happens? Record your results.

Ideas for Supplies ▼

- newspaper
- eggs
- soft materials such as newspaper, Styrofoam, or cotton balls
- tape

WHAT DO YOU THINK OF THE PLANS FOR MY "SUPER EGG HELMET 5000"?

THE WORD THAT COMES TO MIND IS OVERKILL.

To investigate more, use one of the helmet designs that protected the egg and increase the height of your drop. What happens? Why? How can you improve upon the helmet design to better protect the egg from this height?

KEEP A DREAM DIARY

What are your dreams like? Keeping a dream diary is a great way to see if there are patterns to how you sleep and dream.

- **Create a sleep log in a notebook.** Every day, you are going to record the time you went to bed, when you wake up, how many hours you slept, if you remember any dreams, and how you feel each morning.

- **Every night, put your notebook and pen by your bed.** When you wake up, immediately write down everything you remember about your dreams. When writing about your dreams, consider the following.

  1. Are your dreams in color?

  2. How many different dreams do you remember?

  3. Do the same people, places, or events occur in different dreams?

  4. Does eating certain food for dinner affect your dreams that night?

  5. Do you dream differently when you go to bed at different times?

  6. Does the month or season affect your dreams?

  7. Do you have the same dream repeatedly?

- **After several weeks of recording your sleep and dreams, review your records.** What patterns do you see? Can you make any conclusions from your log?

> To investigate more, ask several friends and family members to keep their own dream diaries. After several weeks, compare everyone's experiences. How are they the same? How are they different? What conclusions can you make based on the results?

VOCAB LAB

Write down what you think each word means: **omega-3 fatty acids, antioxidants, addiction, euphoria, impairment, dementia, concussion.**

Discuss your definitions with friends using real-life examples. Did you all come up with the same definitions? Turn to the text and the glossary if you need help.

DOES EXERCISE HELP YOUR BRAIN?

Scientists believe that regular exercise helps to keep your brain cells healthy and working efficiently. Exercise stimulates nerve cells to produce chemicals called neurotrophic factors. These chemicals act like fertilizer for the brain and encourage brain cells to grow and connect with other neurons. Aerobic exercise also stimulates the brain to release other chemicals, such as adrenaline and noradrenaline, which temporarily alert the brain's processing systems.

Exercise can lead to improved mental focus and better decision making. It can reduce the risk of dementia as the brain ages. In this activity, you will set up an experiment to test the effect of exercise on brain function.

- **Before your volunteers arrive, collect 50 small items.** Place 25 on one table and cover them completely with a towel or sheet. Place the second group of 25 different items on a second table and cover with a towel or sheet.

Ideas for Supplies ▼

- 50 small items from around your house, separated into two groups of 25
- 2 tables
- 2 towels or sheets
- paper
- pencils
- several volunteers, split into two groups
- deck of cards
- timer
- exercise props, such as jump ropes

HOW'S IT GOING OVER THERE?

- **Separate your volunteers into group one and group two.** Explain to both groups that they will be taking a memory test. Pass out paper and pencils to each volunteer. Have each volunteer label the paper with his or her name and group number.

- **Remove the towel from the items on table one.** Allow all the volunteers to study the items for one minute. Cover the items again. Give the volunteers three minutes to write down as many items as they remember.

- **For the next 10 minutes, have group one sit down and play cards.** Group two should spend the time performing an aerobic activity, such as jumping jacks, jumping rope, or running in place.

- **After the 10 minutes have ended, remove the towel from the items on table two.** Allow all the volunteers to study the items for one minute. Cover the items again. Give the volunteers three minutes to write down as many items as they remember.

- **Collect the lists and total the number of correct items on each sheet for each person in the first and second memory tests.** How did the exercisers perform on the second memory test compared to the first test? How did they compare to the first group? What conclusions can you make about exercise and the brain?

To investigate more, add a third group of volunteers to the experiment. This group should perform strength exercises during the 10-minute break between memory tests. These could include weight lifting and squats. How does the third group's results compare to the inactive group and the aerobic exercise group? How can you explain your results?

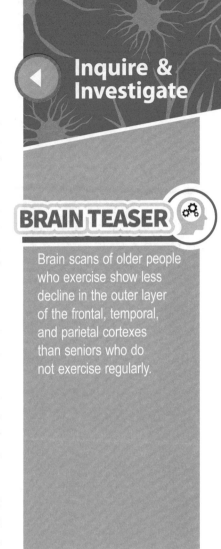

Inquire & Investigate

BRAIN TEASER

Brain scans of older people who exercise show less decline in the outer layer of the frontal, temporal, and parietal cortexes than seniors who do not exercise regularly.

HOW AM I SUPPOSED TO REMEMBER ANYTHING WHEN I'M EXHAUSTED?

STRESS AND THE BRAIN

Stress is a major part of many peoples' lives. You might feel stress about school, friends, parents, work, or the future. How does all this stress affect your brain? In this activity, you will set up an experiment to test the effect of stress on brain function.

Ideas for Supplies ▼

- 50 small items from around your house, separated into two groups of 25
- 2 tables
- 2 towels or sheets
- paper
- pencils
- several volunteers
- ticking timer or clock
- buzzer

To investigate more, design a different way to introduce stress into a memory test. Give your stress test to a group of volunteers. What are your results?

- Before your volunteers arrive, place 25 of the items on one table and cover them with a towel or sheet. Place the second group of 25 different items on a second table and cover them with a towel or sheet.

- Pass out paper and pencils to each volunteer and explain that they will be taking a memory test. Have each volunteer label the paper with his or her name and test number. Tell the volunteers that they will have one minute to study the items and three minutes to write down what they can remember.

- Remove the towel from the items on table one. Allow the volunteers to study the items for one minute. Cover the items again. Give the volunteers three minutes to write down as many items as they remember from the first table.

- Repeat the memory test using the second group of items. This time, play a loudly ticking clock as the volunteers study the items, and again as they write. Sound the buzzer when the time is up for studying the items, and again when the period has ended for writing them down.

- Collect the papers and total the number of correct items on each sheet for each person in the first and second memory tests. How did the volunteers perform on the second memory test compared to the first test? What conclusions can you make about stress and the brain based on this experiment?

A BRAIN OF THE FUTURE

As scientists learn how the brain works, they use this knowledge to develop artificial brains, mind-reading technology, bionic limbs, and other technologies that interact with our brains. For example, scientists are working on a bionic eye that may soon be able to help blind people see.

In this project, you will design your own brain technology. Design a technology that could be used by the government, schools, or yourself.

- **Decide what type of brain technology you would like to create.** For inspiration, research ideas and technologies on the Internet. What kind of problem do you think could be solved by a new brain technology?

- **Once you have decided what type of technology you would like to create, answer the following questions.** How will the technology work? Why did you design it? What need does it fill? Will it be used by government, schools, or individuals? How will it be used? Write down your answers.

- **Create an illustration or model of your technology.** Think about what drawbacks or problems could arise because of the new technology. Will these problems and complications hurt others? If so, how? What other risks exist because of your technology? Do you think the benefits of your new technology outweigh the risks? Why or why not?

> **To investigate more,** take the position of a group that opposes your new technology. Create an argument against creating the technology. What opposition points are the most convincing?

BRAIN TEASER

The bionic eye under development has a computer chip that sits in the back of a person's eye socket and is linked to a tiny video camera built into a pair of glasses. The camera captures images and sends them to the chip, where they are transformed into electrical impulses. These electrical impulses are sent to the visual cortex through the optic nerve.

GLOSSARY

abstract thinking: the final and most complex stage of cognitive thinking. Thinking in terms of concepts and general principles.

action potential: a brief pulse of electrical current that is generated by a neuron.

adapt: to make a change to become better suited to environment.

addictive: causing a strong and harmful need to regularly have or do something.

adrenaline: a hormone produced in high-stress situations. Also called epinephrine.

aerobic: exercise that results in the body circulating more oxygen.

Alzheimer's disease: a form of dementia that grows worse over time and affects memory, thinking, and behavior.

ambidextrous: able to use the right and left hands equally well.

amnesia: a type of severe memory loss.

amputate: to cut off a limb.

amygdala: a structure in the limbic system that has an important role in processing fear response and emotion.

analyze: to examine methodically.

anatomy: the science of the structure of living things.

anterior: the front portion of the brain.

antioxidant: a substance that protects body cells from damage from oxidation.

anxiety: a feeling of fear or uneasiness about possible misfortune. In some cases, anxiety is a mental disorder.

aphasia: a condition that affects the ability to understand or express language, usually because of an injury or stroke.

arachnoid layer: the middle layer of the three meninges that cover and protect the brain.

arcuate fasciculus: a band of nerve fibers that connect Broca's area and Wernicke's area, where language processing occurs.

arousal: to be stimulated to action.

association: a link between two things.

attention deficit disorder: a condition that causes inattentiveness, dreaminess, and passiveness.

auditory: related to receiving and processing sound information.

autism: a serious developmental disorder that affects the ability to communicate and interact with others.

automatic response: a reflex or reflexive action.

autonomic nervous system: regulates the function of internal organs such as the heart, stomach, and intestines.

axon: a fiber-like extension of a neuron that carries electrical signals to other neurons.

basal ganglia: a bundle of cells in the base of the forebrain that is involved with movement.

behavior: the way a person acts or conducts himself.

biology: a branch of science that studies living things.

bionic: an artificial body part that uses electronics.

bipolar disorder: a mental disorder associated with mood swings ranging from depressive lows to manic highs.

blood pressure: the pressure exerted by circulating blood on the walls of blood vessels.

brain: the organ that serves as the center of the body's nervous system.

brain imaging: imaging that uses various techniques to either directly or indirectly image the structure and/or function of the nervous system, also known as neuroimaging.

brain stem: the lower part of the brain that connects to the spinal cord, responsible for basic life-support functions.

breathing rate: the number of breaths taken per minute.

Broca's area: an area in the frontal lobe that is involved with articulating speech.

cell: the basic building block of all living organisms.

central nervous system: the brain and the spinal cord.

cerebellum: an area of the brain located behind the cerebrum that helps regulate posture, balance, and coordination.

cerebral cortex: the outer, wrinkled part of the brain, where most higher-level processing occurs.

cerebral hemispheres: the two halves of the brain.

cerebrospinal fluid: fluid that cushions and protects the brain and spinal cord and provides nutrients to brain tissue.

cerebrum: the major part of the brain, where most higher-level functions and processing occur.

characteristic: an identifying feature or quality of a person, place, or thing.

chemical message: a compound that serves to transmit a message in the body, such as a neurotransmitter or hormone.

chemical reaction: a process in which two or more molecules interact and the molecules change.

chemistry: the science of the properties of substances and how substances react with one another.

chromosomes: parts of a cell that contain genes.

cingulate gyrus: part of the limbic system that helps regulate emotion and pain.

cochlea: the spiral-shaped part of the inner ear that changes sound input into nerve messages that are sent to the brain.

cognitive processes: conscious and unconscious brain processes such as perceiving, thinking, learning, and remembering information.

compensate: to make up for something.

compound: a substance made up of two or more elements.

complex: having many connected parts.

concussion: an injury to the brain caused by hitting the head very hard.

conditioned emotional response: an emotional response that usually results from the association of a relatively neutral stimulus with a painful or fear-inducing experience.

congenital analgesia: a rare condition in which a person does not experience pain.

conscious: perceiving or noticing with controlled thought and observation.

consolidation: the process of strengthening long-term memories.

context cue: information from the environment that can help a person recall a memory.

contract: to decrease in size.

coronal section: a vertical slice through the brain.

corpus callosum: a thick band of nerve tissue that connects the right and left hemispheres of the brain and sends messages between them.

cortex: the outer layer of the cerebrum.

cortisol: a hormone produced in response to stress.

craniotomy: a surgery to remove part of the skull to expose the brain.

data: facts or pieces of information.

deficit: a shortage of something.

degeneration: the process of decaying.

delinquent: a young person who repeatedly breaks the law.

dementia: a brain condition that interferes with thinking and memory.

dendrites: branches on a neuron that receive messages from other neurons and deliver them to the main body of the nerve cell.

deoxyribonucleic acid: the substance that carries your genetic information, the "blueprint" of who you are. It is also known as DNA.

depression: a common mental illness that causes a low mood and sadness.

depth perception: being able to tell how close or far away something is.

developmental disorder: a condition that is characterized by delays in development.

dilation: the act of stretching a part of the body, such as the pupil or a blood vessel.

disorder: a physical or mental condition that is not normal or healthy.

dominant: stronger or more controlling than another.

dopamine: a neurotransmitter that produces feelings of pleasure.

dura mater: the top layer of the meninges that covers the brain inside the skull.

GLOSSARY

dyslexia: a learning disorder characterized by difficulty reading.

electroencephalography (EEG): a recording of the electrical activity of the brain, made by attaching electrodes to the scalp.

element: a pure substance that contains only one kind of atom.

emotion: a strong feeling.

emotional contagion: when a person shares the emotions of another person.

empathy: the ability to share the feelings of another person.

encode: the process of converting a short-term memory into a long-term memory that can be stored in the brain and recalled later.

endorphins: any of a group of peptides occurring in the brain and other body tissues that react with the brain's opiate receptors to raise the pain threshold.

epigenetic alteration: changes in gene expression.

epilepsy: a brain disorder in which nerve cell activity in the brain is disturbed, causing seizures.

epinephrine: a hormone produced in high-stress situations. Also called adrenaline.

episodic: a type of explicit long-term memory that stores personal experiences.

euphoria: a feeling of excitement and happiness.

excitatory: something that triggers or increases a neuron's firing.

explicit memory: memories that can be consciously retrieved and remembered.

expression: the process by which information in a gene is used to produce a protein or other gene product.

extroverted: an outgoing person.

false memory: a phenomenon in which a person remembers an event that did not actually occur.

fear response: an instinctive reaction to a potentially dangerous situation.

fight-or-flight: the brain's response to defend itself against or flee from a perceived threat.

fine motor control: skills needed to perform smaller movements.

fissures: deep clefts on the surface of the brain.

folic acid: a B vitamin that helps the body make healthy new cells.

frequency: the rate or number of times per second that a sound wave cycles.

frontal lobe: the area in the front of the brain that is responsible for thinking, making judgments, planning, decision making, and conscious emotions.

function: how something works. To work or operate in a particular, correct way.

functional imaging: techniques that allow the scientist to measure and show neural activity as visual images.

ganglia: a mass of nerve tissue outside the central nervous system.

gelatinous: jelly-like.

gender: male or female.

genes: sections of DNA that code for a particular trait.

genetic: traits that are passed from parent to child in the DNA.

glial cells: brain cells that support neurons by providing nutrients and removing waste.

glucose: a sugar molecule created in the body by processing starch.

gyri: bulges of tissue on the surface of the brain.

habit: a routine of behavior that happens repeatedly and often unconsciously.

hemisphere: either of the two halves of the brain.

hertz: cycles per second.

high-functioning: able to perform complex tasks even while suffering from a disorder, illness, or advanced age.

higher mental processes: functions that require conscious thought such as language, memory, thinking, attention, abstraction, and perception.

hippocampus: a structure in the limbic system that is critical for encoding and retrieving long-term memories.

horizon: a direction that runs parallel with the skyline.

horizontal section: a slice of the brain that runs parallel with the horizon.

hormone: a chemical messenger that regulates the activity of cells.

hypothalamus: an area of the brain that produces hormones that control many body functions, including hunger, thirst, mood, and emotion.

image: a picture created by imaging technology.

imaging technology: the application of materials, equipment, and methods to create images of the brain and body.

impaired: weakened or damaged.

implicit memory: memories that are not retrieved consciously, but are activated by a particular skill or action, such as tying shoelaces or riding a bike.

impulsive: acting without thinking about consequences.

inferior: an area that is located near the bottom of the brain or below another structure.

information processing: gathering, analyzing, classifying, storing, and retrieving information.

inhibition: slowed or stopped neurons from firing.

inhibitory: something that slows or stops neurons from firing.

innate: inborn or natural.

instinctive: a natural impulse.

intelligence: a person's capacity for logic, abstract thought, understanding, self-awareness, communication, learning, emotional knowledge, memory, planning, creativity, and problem solving.

interpret: to translate or explain.

involuntary: a reflex or action that occurs without conscious direction.

involuntary muscles: muscles that contract without conscious direction, such as the heart.

iris: the part of the eye in which the pupil is located.

judgment: a conscious decision or conclusion.

larynx: the part of the throat that holds the vocal cords.

lateral: an area located on the side of the brain.

lateralization: the localization of a function or activity on one side of the brain or body.

learning disability: a condition such as attention deficit disorder or dyslexia that causes difficulty in processing information and interferes with a person's ability to learn.

left-brain dominance: when the left side of the brain has greater control over a function than the right side.

lesion: an abnormality in the brain that can be seen through brain imaging tests.

limbic system: a group of brain structures located near the inner border of the cortex that have an important role for emotion and memory.

literal: the basic meaning of words.

lobe: one of the four main areas of the brain.

lobotomy: an operation to treat some mental disorders in which part of the brain is cut.

logical: in a way that is orderly and makes sense.

long-term memory: stored information that lasts days, weeks, or years.

long-term potentiation: a change in a neuron that makes it more likely to fire with a group of neurons that it has fired with in the past.

macromolecule: a large molecule, usually made of at least 100 atoms.

mammal: a classification of animals that have hair, three middle ear bones, mammary glands, and a neocortex. Mammals are different from reptiles and birds.

manual dexterity: the ability to use the hands to perform difficult tasks quickly and skillfully.

medial: located near the midline or toward the middle of the brain.

membrane: a thin covering.

memory: the process in which information is encoded, stored, and retrieved.

meninges: three layers of protective tissue between the brain and the skull.

mental function: everything a person can do with their mind including perception, thinking, and memory.

GLOSSARY

mental health: a state of psychological well-being.

metabolic: related to metabolism.

metabolism: a set of chemical reactions within the cells of living things that allow them to grow, reproduce, maintain their structure, and respond to the environment.

mid-sagittal section: a slice of the brain that divides the right and left hemispheres.

mimic: to copy the actions of something.

mind: the thoughts, feelings, beliefs, and intentions that arise from the brain's processes.

mirror neurons: neurons that fire during a familiar action and when thinking of or observing others performing it.

mnemonic: a tool, pattern, or association used to help remember something.

molecule: a unit of matter consisting of two or more atoms.

mood: a state of mind or predominant emotion.

moral: ethical and honest behavior.

motor function: the movement of muscles to perform a specific act.

movement: the act of changing physical location or position or of having this changed.

mutation: a permanent change in an organism's DNA.

myelin sheath: a fatty material that surrounds and insulates the axons of some neurons.

nature: a result of innate qualities.

negativity bias: the tendency of humans to better recall bad memories than good memories.

neocortex: the wrinkled outer layer of the brain, also called the cerebral cortex.

nerve: a fiber that transmits messages from the brain to the body and vice versa.

nervous system: the communication system of the body, made of nerve cells that connect the brain and extend through the body.

neural circuit: a functional group of interconnected neurons that create a neural pathway.

neural networks: connected networks of neurons in the brain.

neurogenesis: the process by which new neurons are generated.

neurologist: a medical doctor that diagnoses and treats disorders of the brain and nervous system.

neurology: a branch of medicine that deals with the brain and nervous system.

neuron: a cell of the nervous system that sends messages to others by generating and passing electrical signals. Also called a nerve cell.

neuroscience: the scientific study of the brain and nervous system.

neurotransmitter: a chemical secreted by neurons that carries signals across a synapse to another neuron.

norepinephrine: a neurotransmitter that is secreted in response to stress.

nucleus: the part of the cell that controls how it functions.

nucleus accumbens: a part of the brain associated with pleasurable sensation.

nurture: to care for and encourage the development of something.

nutrients: the substances in food that living things need to live and grow.

objective reality: the reality that exists independent of a person's mind or perception.

occipital lobe: an area in the back of the cerebrum responsible for visual processing.

olfactory: relating to or connected with the sense of smell.

olfactory bulb: the brain's smell center, located in the limbic area.

olfactory fatigue: when you stop smelling an odor after being exposed to it for a period of time.

olfactory receptors: receptors in the nasal cavity that send electric signals to the olfactory bulb when activated by scent molecules.

omega-3 fatty acids: substances found in certain foods such as salmon and walnuts that promote brain health.

optic chiasm: the point at which the optic nerves from each eye meet and cross over.

optic nerve: a bundle of nerve fibers that carry signals from the retina to the brain for processing.

optic radiation: a thick bundle of axons used to relay signals from the thalamus to the primary visual cortex.

optical illusion: a visually perceived image that differs from objective reality.

organ: a part of the body that serves a specific function.

organism: any living thing, such as a plant or animal.

ossicles: small bones inside the ear that vibrate with sound.

oxygen: a chemical element with the symbol O.

papillae: little bumps on the tongue that contain clusters of taste buds.

parietal lobe: an area of the brain near the top and back of the head, mainly involved with spatial awareness, body orientation, and attention.

Parkinson's disease: a disorder of the central nervous system that affects movement, often including tremors.

perception: the ability to interpret information from the senses.

peripheral nervous system: the part of the nervous system that includes all of the nerves and neurons outside the brain and spinal cord.

personality: the characteristics and ways of behaving that make people different from each other.

perspective: a person's point of view.

phantom limb: the sensation that a missing limb is still attached to the body.

phenomenon: something that is impressive or extraordinary.

philosopher: a person who studies truth, wisdom, the nature of reality, and knowledge.

photoreceptor: a specialized neuron in the eye that transforms light waves into nerve signals that are sent to the brain.

phrenology: a belief popular in the nineteenth century that personal characteristics and mental abilities could be learned from the bumps on a person's skull.

physiology: the study of the internal workings of living organisms. Physiology is a branch of biology.

pia mater: the layer of the meninges that is closest to the brain.

plasticity: the ability of the brain to change its structure and function.

posterior: the back portion of the brain.

posture: the position of your body when you stand, walk, or sit.

prefrontal cortex: the area of the brain located in the anterior frontal lobe that is responsible for reasoning, planning, judgment, empathy, abstract ideas, and conscience.

preserve: to protect something so that it stays in its original state.

pressure: the exertion of a force on a surface by an object, fluid, or air that is in contact with it.

priority: something that is more important than other things.

prism: a transparent solid body, often having triangular bases, used for dispersing light into a spectrum or for reflecting rays of light.

procedural memory: the part of long-term memory responsible for remembering how to do things.

process: an activity that takes several steps to complete.

proprioception: sensory neurons that are responsible for the sense of self and the awareness of body position and movement.

proteins: nutrients that are essential to the growth and repair of tissue.

pruning: the cutting back of neural fibers that occurs in the brain's development around age four.

protrusion: something that sticks out.

psychological: pertaining to or affecting the mind.

GLOSSARY

psychologist: a specialist who studies the mind and behavior and provides mental health care.

psychology: the science of the mind and behavior.

radioactive marker: a radioactive substance that is attached to a molecule so scientists can trace that molecule through the body.

rapid eye movement (REM): a phase of sleep characterized by rapid eye movements and vivid dreams.

rash: acting without thinking.

receptor: an end organ or a group of end organs of sensory neurons, specialized to be sensitive to stimulating agents, such as touch or heat.

reconstruction: the act of rebuilding something.

regulate: to control or adjust to keep at a certain standard.

REM sleep: a stage in the sleep cycle when dreams occur and memories are organized.

reptilian: like a reptile.

retina: the part of the eye containing light-sensitive cells that send electrical signals to the visual area of the brain for processing.

retrieval: to recall or locate a memory in storage.

right-brain dominance: when the right side of the brain has greater control over a function than the left side.

rigidity: being stiff and difficult to change.

rotating: turning around a center point or axis.

saturated fat: a type of animal or vegetable fat that tends to increase cholesterol levels in the blood.

schizophrenia: a brain disorder in which people interpret reality abnormally.

secrete: to produce a liquid.

semantic: a type of explicit long-term memory that deals with general facts and information.

sensation: the brain's awareness of a stimulus.

sense organ: a specialized body structure that receives or is sensitive to internal or external stimuli.

senses: the ability of a living thing to learn about its surroundings. Sight, hearing, touch, taste, and smell are the five senses.

sensory: relating to sensation or the physical senses.

sensory inputs: environmental stimuli that are detected by the senses.

sensory receptors: specialized neurons in the sense organs that detect stimuli and send messages to the brain.

serotonin: a neurotransmitter that regulates functions, including mood, appetite, and sensory perception.

short-term memory: a phase of memory in which a limited amount of information may be held for several seconds to minutes. Sometimes called working memory.

significance: importance.

skull: the bony framework of the head that protects the brain.

social skills: the personal skills needed for successful social communication and interaction.

somatosensory cortex: the area of the brain that processes input from various receptors in the body that are sensitive to touch.

spatial: relating to space and the relationship of objects within it.

spatial awareness: the ability to be aware of your position in space.

species: a class of organisms having common characteristics or qualities.

spherical: shaped round, like a ball.

spinal cord: a thick cord of nerve tissue that links the brain to nerves in the rest of the body.

spine: the long row of bones in your back that protect your spinal cord.

stapes: a small, stirrup-shaped bone in the middle ear that vibrates with sound.

stimuli: changes in the environment that cause a reaction from the brain.

storage: to put something away, such as a memory, until it is needed later.

stress: pressure or strain, often due to changes in conditions or environments.

stroke: a lack of oxygen to part of the brain caused by the blocking or breaking of a blood vessel.

structural imaging: creating images of the brain's structures.

structure: the organization and arrangement of tissues, parts, or organs.

sulci: grooves in the brain's surface.

superior: an area that is located near the top of the brain or above another structure.

surface area: a measure of the total area that the surface of an object occupies.

synapse: a gap between two neurons through which communication occurs.

synesthesia: a condition in which one sense is stimulated and it is perceived at the same time by another sense or senses.

taste bud: a cluster of nerve endings on the tongue and in the lining of the mouth that senses taste.

technology: the use of science and engineering to do things such as medical processes and research.

temporal lobe: an area of the brain on the side of the head involved with hearing, language, and memory.

tension: mental or emotional strain.

thalamus: a pair of structures between the brain stem and the cerebrum that act as a relay station for sensory information entering the brain.

tissue: a group or mass of similar cells working together to perform common functions.

traits: features or qualities that make somebody or something recognizable.

trans fat: a type of unsaturated fat that is uncommon in nature but can be created artificially.

trauma: damage caused by physical harm from an external source.

traumatic brain injury: physical damage to the brain caused by an external source.

tremor: a shaking or trembling movement.

trigger: anything that serves as a stimulus to start a reaction or response.

tympanic membrane: a thin membrane separating the middle ear from the auditory canal, also called the eardrum.

umami: a savory taste that is found in fish, cured meats, and aged cheese, among other foods.

unconscious: occurring without awareness.

ventricle: a space within the brain that holds cerebrospinal fluid.

verbal: relating to words and speech.

vibrate: to move to and fro or up and down quickly and repeatedly.

vibration: the act of vibrating.

visual: relating to sight.

voluntary muscles: muscles that are controlled by conscious thought, such as when you throw a ball.

vulnerable: susceptible to emotional or physical harm.

Wernicke's area: an area in the temporal lobe that is responsible for understanding language.

white blood cells: blood cells that are part of the body's immune system. They protect against infection by destroying diseased cells and germs.

white matter: brain tissue beneath the cortex, made of densely packed axons that carry signals to other neurons.

withdrawal: to take something away.

working memory: see short-term memory.

zones: areas.

METRIC CONVERSIONS

Use this chart to find the metric equivalents to the English measurements in this activity. If you need to know a half measurement, divide by two. If you need to know twice the measurement, multiply by two. How do you find a quarter measurement? How do you find three times the measurement?

English	Metric
1 inch	2.5 centimeters
1 foot	30.5 centimeters
1 yard	0.9 meter
1 mile	1.6 kilometers
1 pound	0.5 kilogram
1 teaspoon	5 milliliters
1 tablespoon	15 milliliters
1 cup	237 milliliters

RESOURCES

⊙ Books

Brain: The Complete Mind by Michael S. Sweeney
National Geographic, 2009.

Brainworks: The Mind-Bending Science of How You See, What You Think, and Who You Are by Michael S. Sweeney
National Geographic, 2011.

The Human Brain Book by Rita Carter
DK Publishing, 2014.

⊙ Websites

BrainFacts.org
www.brainfacts.org
This site, which is reviewed by scientists, seeks to inform about exciting new discoveries in the realm of brain science and provide resources for students and teachers to learn about the brain.

Neuroscience for Kids
faculty.washington.edu/chudler/neurok.html

⊙ Museums and Places to Visit

"Brain: The Inside Story," American Museum of Natural History
www.amnh.org/exhibitions/past-exhibitions/brain-the-inside-story
The museum's online exhibit explores the way the human brain works, including senses, emotions, thinking, aging, and brains of the future.

"Your Brain," The Franklin Institute
www.fi.edu/exhibit/your-brain
Visitors to the institute can climb through a two-story-tall neural network with lighting and sound effects.

⊙ QR Code Index

Page 16: www.youtu.be/cn1qVZF-bl4

Page 18: www.youtube.com/watch?v=O-3j2zUX8zs

Page 20: www.dana.org/uploadedImages/Images/neuroanatomy_large.jpg

Page 22: www.youtube.com/watch?v=p5zFgT4aofA

Page 26: www.archive.org/details/cerebrianatomecu00will

Page 28: www.technologyreview.com/featuredstory/526501/brain-mapping

Page 36: www.goo.gl/0Q40E6

Page 72: www.einstein.yu.edu/news/releases/968/watching-molecules-morph-into-memories

Page 82: www.mathsisfun.com/games/memory

Page 88: www.youtube.com/watch?v=zt9S2r64QuQ

Page 97: www.newscenter.berkeley.edu/2011/03/08/sleep-brainwaves

INDEX